Memoirs of A Geriatric Ski Bum

Memoirs of A Geriatric Ski Bum

Stanley Hirsch

To order additional copies of this book, contact:
Xlibris Corporation
1-888-795-4274
www.Xlibris.com
Orders@Xlibris.com
102229

CONTENTS

To Uncle Jack,

who opened up so many worlds to me,
including skiing

ACKNOWLEDGMENTS

A book such as this is born in part through the people who have crossed one's path over the years. Many have been brought forward within the pages of this book; others have been silent behind the scenes. It is these silent participants who have made a strong contribution to its completion.

My deep appreciation to Miguel Ethel, who inspired me to write this in the first place; to my editor and critic Joan Ostroff, whose expertise has been exceptional; and to my lifelong friend Victor Goldin, who encouraged, supported, and applauded what has been, for me, a joyous effort.

Of the many who have enriched my life both on and off the ski slopes, I give special recognition to Michael and Sonja Munte, Hank Deutsch, and Jerald Hunsacker.

Oh, it's a long, long while from May to December
But the days grow short when you reach September.
When the autumn weather turns the leaves to flame
One hasn't got time for the waiting game.

—Maxwell Anderson

PROLOGUE

A VERY SPECIAL LOVE AFFAIR

I was helicopter skiing in the Canadian Rockies when I was killed by an avalanche. I was ninety-three years old.

When I awoke the following morning, Christmas Day, it was snowing in Val d'Isère (France).

The dream was not really a nightmare. One can only hope that when it comes, at any age, the final exit will not be one of prolonged suffering. If this "last run" happens while skiing, something you love to do, then it could truly be a blessing.

I related the dream to a psychiatrist friend whom I ski with in Snowbird, Utah. He said, "You've got it made! When you're ninety-three, don't go to Canada!"

Though it might seem frivolous to a nonskier, this gave me a goal—to still be skiing when I'm ninety-three. As of this writing, I have nine years to go.

I have skied over 1,500 days in the past thirty-nine years, having skied for the first time at the age of forty-five. Clearly, I felt the need to catch up for having started so late in life; and I therefore ski whenever the opportunity presents itself. Now, in addition to more than fifty resorts in the Alps, I have skied in Argentina, Chile, New Zealand, Canada, and in most of the major resorts in the United States, both East and West.

In this book, I will relate some stories about many of these resorts, both skiing and nonskiing memorabilia, and some involving notable personalities, all of whom share an addiction to skiing. These will include former champions Pepi Gramshammer, Junior Bounous, Ingemar Stenmark, and Vicente Vera. I will also outline some of the techniques I was privileged to have learned from them, which might have greater significance for older skiers. How these champions have handled aging and continue to enjoy skiing is an inspiration to all of any age.

Yes, there are other very interesting personalities: a racing coach from Val d'Isère; a ski instructor in France whose home is Brooklyn, New York; Warren Miller on Orcas Island; a skier in Snowbird who skis with wings; and the personal pilot of the former Shah of Iran, whom I met when she was on the ski patrol in Corvatsch near St. Moritz.

We have all shared something wonderful—a love for skiing—a very special love affair.

TWO WORLD WARS, AN END,
A WILL, AND THE BEGINNING

On Sunday, November 16, 1941, a commentator on the New York radio station WMCA predicted that the United States would be at war with Japan within three weeks. Exactly three weeks later, on December 7, 1941, the Japanese attacked Pearl Harbor.

The commentator was Burnet Hershey, who had been the youngest person on the Ford Peace Mission during World War I, as well as the youngest reporter at the Versailles Peace Conference, which officially ended what was purported to be the "War to End All Wars." Burnet Hershey was also a founder and subsequently president of the Overseas Press Club. At his memorial service, he was eulogized as a "reporter's reporter" by a fellow club member.

Burnet Hershey in Paris

What does this distinguished journalist and war correspondent, who never skied a day in his life, have to do with a book about skiing? Well, if not for him, this book most likely would never have been written.

Burnet Hershey was the pen name of my Uncle Jack Hirsch, who died on his seventy-fifth birthday in 1971. Married and divorced twice with no children, he had three surviving siblings and many nephews and nieces. He left an ambiguous will and a codicil that he had dictated to his attorney on the phone but never signed. Both the will and the codicil were contested by several members of the family. Found in his files was a carbon copy of a letter to his banker in Lausanne, Switzerland, which clearly stated his wishes.

The unsigned codicil had named me executor of the estate. When I showed the carbon copy of the letter to my attorney, he said, "Stanley, go to Lausanne, don't write, don't call. Go, and get the original of this letter with your uncle's signature, and we'll be able to clear up the estate."

So in April 1972, instead of the usual holiday visit to my parents in Miami, Joan and I took our two boys, Jamie (eight) and Michael (six), to Switzerland on a fly/drive trip.

A Swissair calendar we had in our home had a splendid picture of the Matterhorn. Michael had said he would like to climb it one day, and Joan told him she would take him to see it. So our trip had more than one purpose.

In her younger skiing days, Joan had made many trips to Chamonix (France) and a few to Zermatt (Switzerland), so after arriving in Geneva, we spent our first day in Chamonix, just an hour away. The boys had ski lessons, and we settled for a delightful lunch in the sun.

We then went to Montreux, and I visited the banker in nearby Lausanne. When I showed him the carbon copy of the letter and told him I needed the original in order to clear up the estate, he pulled the original from his files and exchanged it for my carbon copy.

Now that the legal problem was resolved, we went to Zermatt to see the awesome Matterhorn for real. Since Zermatt prohibits automobiles, we drove to St. Niklaus and took our first cog railway ride the rest of the way. But when we arrived in Zermatt, the clouds and fog were so heavy we couldn't see the Matterhorn or any other mountain. We decided to stay overnight; how could we come this far without achieving our purpose?

Later that afternoon, we saw hundreds of skiers descending the mountain. Skiing? Well, why not? Once the decision was made, we went to the ski school to arrange for instruction the next day, and then to a shop to rent the equipment. Joan hadn't skied for years, so we were all at the novice level—second time for the boys and first time for me.

The next morning, we awoke to a downpour. I said to our instructor, who was waiting in the lobby of our hotel, "You don't ski in the rain, do you?" She replied, "It's not raining where we're going."

We boarded the Gornergratbahn, another cog railway that ascends the major mountain in Zermatt. It has many stations, servicing all levels of skiing. As we rode, the rain changed to a lovely, gentle snowfall. We got off at Riffelberg, an intermediate stop. (It now seems strange that the first ski lift I ever took was a train!) Most of the morning was spent with us continuously falling into about six inches of white fluff as we learned to snowplow and sideslip.

The author with his sons at Riffelberg

Just before noon, it stopped snowing, the clouds parted, and the sun emerged. Jamie pointed to the sky. "LOOK!" There, between two banks of clouds, against the bluest sky I had ever seen, was what we had come to see—the Matterhorn!

It isn't easy to describe the simultaneous sensations of awe and exhilaration one feels when first seeing this colossus. It is a majestic, natural sculpture reaching to the sky, unlike any other mountain you have seen or will ever see.

At noon, skiers came down to the restaurant nearby. After lunch, there in the middle of the snowy Alps, men stripped to the waist and women to their bathing suits. They were sunbathing with their ski boots on. We were hooked and made reservations to return that Christmas.

That was thirty-nine years ago, just after my forty-fifth birthday, and I've returned to ski resorts in the Alps once or twice a year since then—in France, Austria, Italy, Germany and, of course, Switzerland.

The original letter with Burnet Hershey's signature settled the estate. I will be forever grateful to my Uncle Jack. His will became the major reason for our first trip to Switzerland which led to so many more family skiing trips throughout the years.

It is remarkable that the end of his fulfilled life should have led to the beginning of a thrilling life of skiing for us all. Thanks so much, Uncle Jack!

THE NUMBERS GAME

As I walked out of the funeral parlor, I heard that same old, tired cliché, "Well, when your number's up, your number's up." With an aging skier's acumen and a bit of disdain, I said, "You guys were all crazy. You took numbers!"

Numbers? Older skiers battle numbers every day, from the beginning to the end of every ski trip. Let's look at some of them.

Altitude! Skiing at an altitude of eleven thousand to twelve thousand feet isn't a problem at a younger age. As the years progress, oxygen levels may cause problems for older skiers, both during skiing and at the base areas. They may limit their skiing to eight thousand or nine thousand feet and base areas to five thousand to six thousand feet.

Climate! When we were younger, we skied as long as the temperature was above zero and, sometimes, even below. Now if it's below ten degrees, we play bridge.

Preparation! Getting ready for skiing each day, sorting out gear, donning layers of clothing, adjusting ski boot buckles, etc.? It used to take no more than thirty minutes. Now it takes at least forty-five and often as much as an hour.

Stamina! Years ago, I would be on the first ski lift at 9:30, ski till 12:30, have lunch, and ski again until the lifts closed—a total of five to six hours. Now you'll find me on the first lift at 10:00, taking a coffee break at 11:30, lunch at 1:30, and just maybe I'll ski till 3:00—a total of two-and-a-half to three hours.

Skis! It used to be that the length of skis was considered a mark of the skier's ability: the longer the ski, the better the skier. However, as the design of skis changed to a more parabolic shape with wider shovels (front) and wider tails (back), providing more ski surface at shorter lengths, longer skis don't have the same significance as before. Even though, as I got older, I reduced the length of my skis from 200 cm to 180 cm, I was enlightened even further a few years ago when I unexpectedly met an instructor friend, Mark Smith from New Zealand, on a chairlift in Vail. Mark asked me what length my skis were. When he heard 180 cm, he said, "Stanley, I'm taller and younger than you, and I'm skiing on 170 cm. You should cut down to at most 160 cm; that will increase the life of your skiing." I'm now on skis measuring 160 cm and enjoying them immensely.

Powder snow! When new snow falls, ski areas report the amount of powder on their slopes in number of inches. Though at a younger age you might have been able to handle fifteen inches of powder with ease, as you grow older, even eight inches presents a challenge. However, since there are variations within powder, this doesn't tell the whole story.

When it snows in Utah and Colorado, what falls is called Champagne Powder, a trademark of the Rockies. It is very dry and light, so light that skiers can *float* through thirty inches of powder with very little effort. If just a fraction of that snow falls in the Lake Tahoe resorts at Squaw Valley, Alpine Meadows, or Heavenly Valley (California and Nevada), it can be laden with moisture, very wet, and known as Sierra Cement. Skiing through just ten inches of that is extremely difficult, regardless of age.

Air! Moguls (bumps) are a nemesis for most intermediate skiers, but advanced skiers can handle them quite well. However, as you age, negotiating them is more tiring: those bumps require concerted technique and verve. In the past, you were able to hit a bump head on, which would lift you into a turn in the air, a jet turn. This is a fascinating turn when you can land and slide into the next mogul. When you're younger, you might be able to lift as much as two feet in the air. As you get older you can still make a jet turn but the "air" is considerably less. That foot of air becomes another number, just an inch or two, but it is still most exhilarating and, in more ways than one, quite uplifting.

At one time, I owned a condo at the Canyon Racquet Club which is near the junction of Big and Little Cottonwood Canyons near Salt Lake City, Utah. It led to years of skiing at Snowbird as well as Alta, Solitude, and Brighton. After about five years, I sold it to another Long Islander, and we skied together quite often. Actually, after selling Jonathan the condo, I went to Utah more often as his guest than when I owned it myself.

We skied mainly at Snowbird and became quite friendly with Brent van Buren, one of the managers of the ski shop at the Cliff Lodge. Only once did the three of us ski together. Brent is twenty years younger than Jonathan, who is twenty years my junior. After we got off the tram at the top, we headed for Regulator Johnson, a black run with many moguls. Jonathan and I skied down about half way, stopped and looked up to watch Brent ski down. We had never before seen him ski. He was marvelous, doing short turns down the fall line with amazing grace.

As we stood there, Brent went by and Jonathan, bending his right arm, poked me in the ribs saying, "Gee, if I were only twenty-eight again." After catching my breath, I bent my left arm, my elbow sank into his rib cage and I said, "Boy, if I were only forty-eight again." That was sixteen years ago.

Even if you never "took a number," there will, inevitably, come a time when you will get one. Hopefully, when that number comes up, your exit will be tranquil, peaceful, and a celebration of a life made more joyous by the wonderment and enchantment of skiing.

MAGICAL ZERMATT!

The first place I ever skied has lent a magical tinge to my memories over the years; it has also been, for me, miraculous. The magic will be described now. The miracle? Later!

Of all the more than fifty resorts I have skied in the Alps, Zermatt will always be my favorite. Not because it was the first and not because it has the best skiing terrain, but because it has everything that you would ever dream a ski resort should have—and so much more. If I am ever asked by one who has never skied in the Alps to recommend where to go, I say, without hesitation, "Zermatt!"

Zermatt is nestled in a valley surrounded by twenty-three mountain peaks. The dominant one is the Matterhorn, one of the most famous mountains in the world. From the Swiss side, it is an imposing sculpture created by forces of nature that man could never have imagined. Viewed from a variety of angles within Zermatt, it seems to be everywhere. Almost anywhere you are, the Matterhorn is in your sight. It is truly awesome.

To scale the Matterhorn is one of the great challenges for mountain climbers. In recent times more than three thousand per year make the attempt. There have been many tragedies, including climbers who may have reached the peak but who lost their lives on the descent. One of the most historical places in Zermatt is the cemetery where rest many who didn't return safely. The gravestones, dating back to the nineteenth century, tell the tragic stories.

Private cars are not allowed in Zermatt. All transportation, including buses and taxis, is electric. As you might imagine, the air is as pure as air can be. There is also horse-drawn transport which, very early on, was the *only* transportation in the village. Today, no longer the norm, it provides a charming romantic element.

Commemorative gravestone in Zermatt cemetery

The closest you can come by car is Tasch, about four miles away. You park your car and take the cog railway, built in 1897, to Zermatt, which is at the end of the line.

The southern face of the Matterhorn looks down on the village of Cervinia in Italy, where the mountain is called Monte Cervino. Strangely, viewed from Cervinia, Monte Cervino does not have the distinctive shape of the mountain we know as the Matterhorn. Cervinia was purposely built as a resort in the 1930s and remains one of Europe's highest-elevation ski areas with lifts reaching an altitude of 12,792 feet.

Cervinia and Zermatt are interconnected. From Zermatt, take one gondola and two cable cars to Klein (small) Matterhorn, walk through the man-made tunnel and you will reach the pistes that will take you to Cervinia. On the way, and within walking distance for nonskiers, is an ice cave (grotto), which is part of an immense glacier. Signs warn skiers to return to the groomed piste and not try to "cut a corner" by skiing across the glacier which can be sun-drenched, resulting in the ice not being strong enough to support the weight of a skier. If the ice breaks, one can fall into a crevasse and freeze to death in a short time.

One day, my son Michael and I, on the way to Cervinia, were turning the corner on the groomed piste that encircles the glacier when we encountered a young man walking without either skis or snowboard and holding a cell phone to his ear. We could see that he was in great distress. He was talking with a friend who had attempted to snowboard across the glacier when the ice broke. He had fallen into a crevasse and was unable to climb out.

The young man was Chinese and because of difficulty with the language he was unable to contact the ski patrol by phone. He was now trying to walk back to the Klein Matterhorn Ski Patrol station which would probably have taken him close to an hour, by which time there would have been very little chance that his friend would have survived.

Michael got on his own cell phone and reached the ski patrol. Within a few minutes, a helicopter was dispatched and almost instantly located the crevasse. In a superb effort of delicate maneuvering, they rescued the very cold young man in a miraculously short time. (That night, at our hotel, we were visited by a contingent of young men from Hong Kong. They expressed their gratitude as best they could, thanking Michael for his part in helping to save their friend's life.)

After all this excitement, there was not enough time for a trip to Cervinia, so we put it off until the next day. Instead, we made the eight-mile run with considerable varied terrain back to Zermatt. It is one of the highest and longest runs in the world and displays the incredible diversity of Zermatt skiing.

Cervinia and Zermatt share over seventy ski lifts including the cog railway (the Gornergratbahn), a high-speed underground railway (funicular) known as the Sunnega Express, and seventeen cable cars and six gondolas.

Cervinia, great for heavenly cruising from top to bottom, is a delight for intermediate skiers. It connects to another Italian sector, Valtournenche. The only real danger is finding yourself in Valtournenche too late to get back to Cervinia, which has the only lifts that connect to Zermatt. Well, spending the night in Italy can't be all bad if you can find something to wear to replace your ski boots.

For Zermatt itself, the one word to describe the ski areas is "paradise." There are three basic paradisiacal sectors: Sunnega/Blauherd/Rothorn, Gornergrat, and Klein Matterhorn/Schwarzee. They are all interconnected and offer an immense ski safari to acquaint the newcomer with the vast amount of skiing available.

The ski safari starts with the underground funicular to the Sunnega Paradise, followed by a unique hybrid lift of gondola cars alternating with quad chairs which bring you to the Blauherd Paradise. A panoramic cable car carries you to the peak, the Rothorn Paradise. Now you begin to ski and head back down toward Blauherd and the Sunnega Paradise but, after making a large U-turn and passing a mogul field on the right, a sign on the left directs you to Gant. Instead of heading straight down to Blauherd, you make that left turn into a zigzag run and a schuss that takes you past the restaurant, Fluhalp, and down to Gant. If you were not on the ski safari, the Fluhalp, with its live music and breathtaking views of the Matterhorn, would be great for lunch. But you are on a safari and have to cover as much territory as time will allow. Lunch will come later.

You don't have the luxury of exploring all the runs in each area. The safari is meant to give you an overview. You will not be able to resist the temptation to return at a future time to sample the full menu of each Paradise.

At Gant, there is a gondola that, if you chose, would take you back to Blauherd, the Sunnega Paradise, and the Rothorn Paradise. Instead, you take the new cable car to Hohtälli. There is now a choice between two short cable cars. One goes to the top of Stockhorn, one of the most difficult runs in Zermatt. If you're not an expert skier, the first few turns are absolutely scary. In the many times I've been to Zermatt I've skied it only three times, very carefully.

So you take the other cable car to the top of Gornergrat, to the Gornergrat Kulm Hotel and the top station of the Gornergratbahn. The terrace of the hotel is another great place for lunch, but on safari, you have to keep going. There are many runs down to Riffelberg, the next major station; but instead of going direct, you detour to the right after passing under the small railway bridge. Now you are in more difficult terrain, but one well handled by intermediates; this is another run that shows the great diversity of Zermatt skiing. At the next intersection, another left turn will bring you to the Riffelalp station of the Gornergratbahn. Take the train up to Riffelberg, the next station.

Shun the self-service restaurant at Riffelberg and ski down to another part of Riffelalp. It's now time for lunch, and you have a choice of many restaurants with table service, starting with those at the five-star Hotel Riffelalp and several more as you go down the piste. Generally, the lower you go down the slope, the lower are the restaurant prices.

After lunch, you ski all the way down to the bottom of the valley and reach a two-way gondola. One way goes back up to Riffelberg, but you've been there. The other way goes up to Furi, your introduction to the Klein Matterhorn/Schwarzee sector.

At Furi you take a cable car to Trockener Steg, a center for several lifts and runs. Then the Klein Matterhorn cable car, the walk through the tunnel, and the magnificent beginning of the Matterhorn Glacier Paradise, where you have the option of skiing to Italy or staying on the Swiss side. This is a Zermatt safari, so you stay on the Swiss side and ski the Theodulgletscher back down to Trockener Steg. Had you not had lunch in Riffelalp, midway down to Trockener Steg, with a loop-to-loop schuss off to the right, is the Gandegg Hütte. This mountain restaurant is a must during a stay in Zermatt.

This time you take the chairlifts in the direction of the Plateau Rosa where you will have a choice of gentle cruising or friendly bumps combined with a schuss which will bring you to Furgg. The Schwarzee Paradise will be reached with a rather strange gondola-type lift, each car carrying about twelve standing skiers. If the weather is good, you will be greeted by a blast of gorgeous sunshine, and the views will make you feel as if you were on top of the world.

The runs from the Schwarzee Paradise seem to be endless but there is also something extra. You are now skiing at the base of the Matterhorn and this adds something exceptional—perhaps even spiritual.

A very long run around the sector and a track will bring you back to Furi. This is a good time for a warm-up. No, not for skiing, but for après-skiing. Either the Zum See or the Blatten is there for your thirst and good-fellowship. The skiing ends with a zigzag run and then a schuss to the bus stop. You're back in the village. The safari is finished, but it has given you just a taste of the skiing smorgasbord that is Zermatt. You have only skied groomed runs. The vast amount of off-piste skiing would require another book—and these runs would not be recommended for older skiers.

I must mention the beautiful hotel I have stayed at during most of my trips to Zermatt. The four-star Mirabeau Hotel is one of only three four-star hotels rated in the list of the top thirty Holiday Hotels in all of Switzerland. The other twenty-seven are five-star hotels. The proprietors, Sepp and Rose Julen and their daughter Anna, comprise a family whose personal touch is evident all the time. It is "hands-on" management. The bountiful Raclette served every Tuesday night is traditional. Friday night's dessert buffet is memorable. The Mirabeau's cuisine rivals anything served in the "Palaces."

Many of the five-star hotels have added the word "palace" to their names. For example, the Mont Cervin Hotel is now the Mont Cervin Palace Hotel. The Mirabeau is not palatial. It is too warm and cozy to be called a palace, but it has most of the qualities attributed to those that are. I wouldn't hesitate to call it the Mirabeau Paradise Hotel.

All of the above has detailed the magic of Zermatt. The miracle, for me, was not just the miraculous rescue of the young man on the glacier. It dates back to my unexpected introduction to the world of skiing so long ago, which has given me countless wonderful adventures in the nearly forty years of high-spirited life.

THE GLACIER EXPRESS

To my mind, the most satisfying way to travel through the glistening snows of the Swiss Alps from the charming Hotel Mirabeau in Zermatt to the elegant Palace Hotel in St. Moritz is on the Glacier Express, one of the world's most famous trains on an historic railway.

Known as "the slowest express train in the world," the seven-and-a-half-hour journey connects the two premier Alpine ski resorts with some stops along the way. One of these is at Andermatt, a splendid ski area that's often overlooked. There's also a branch of the Express that goes to Davos.

The route between St. Moritz and Zermatt crosses 291 bridges, goes through ninety-one tunnels, and reaches altitudes of over seven thousand feet. The winter landscape of the extraordinary Swiss countryside is a treat for the eyes, with the beauty of the Rhône Valley and the Rhine Gorge adding to the scenic highlights.

Reservations are necessary for the excellently prepared lunch in the dining car. The delightful experience is similar to dining on an ocean-going liner, but the "sea" is pure white.

Arriving at the St. Moritz train station and being greeted by the chauffeur of the Palace Hotel's Rolls Royce limousine completes a splendid transfer from Zermatt to St. Moritz in keeping with the style of the entire journey.

A stylish welcome to St. Moritz

ST. MORITZ, THE PALACE,
FIRSTS, AND COINCIDENCES

The very name of St. Moritz conjures up thoughts of elegance that other upscale ski resorts such as Megève and Courchevel in France, Cortina in Italy, and Gstaad in Switzerland cannot rival. No other can boast of so many five-star hotels, with one, Badrutt's Palace Hotel, the most legendary of all.

In March, the Palace was the scene of a backgammon tournament attended by many of the world's greatest players. I was relatively new to tournament backgammon, but had had some modest success locally. My wife Joan had read about the tournament which occurred, coincidentally, at the time of her birthday. She suggested we go to the Palace for both skiing and the tournament. Primarily, of course, it was for skiing and her birthday; the tournament was secondary.

However, miraculously, I reached the semifinal round which was to be held, after skiing, Saturday afternoon. I told Joan that if I won the semifinal, I would naturally be in the final late Sunday afternoon. She said, "But we're scheduled to go home on Sunday. We can't change it; I've made too many plans. How was I supposed to know that you would reach the final?"

With a little aplomb and a great deal of irregularity, I made an offer to my semifinal opponent which he couldn't refuse—that we would play the semifinal match on Saturday but, regardless of who won, we would report him as the winner. He would go on to play the final, and we would split whatever prize money was won. Since there was prize money for reaching both the semifinal and the final, we would both win a nice bit of change. He agreed on the condition that he would keep the trophy, the winner's or the runner's-up.

I beat him in the semifinal, but he went on to play the final, which he lost. He sent me half of the runner-up money and kept the trophy.

It was a marvelous holiday and, as we left the Palace on Sunday, Joan said, "From now on, your birthday gift problems for me are over. Just take me to the Palace in St. Moritz."

After many years, we became regulars at the Palace, where there was a pecking order in the dining room. Though we didn't have the highest of elite qualifications, our seating was in the most favorable location. Perhaps it was because Bianchi, the head waiter, liked to ski with me.

Additionally, we received some preferential treatment, such as being invited for dinner by the hotel manager. This was somewhat akin to being invited to dine at the captain's table on a cruise. We became quite friendly with Max Keller, the manager, and his wife, Irina. He often made the point that, if one brought his wife to St. Moritz, they might stay at one of the other five-star hotels such as the Suvretta House or the Kulm. However, if someone brought his girlfriend, the couple would stay at the Palace.

If we were to have dinner with Max and Irina, we usually met at the bar at about 8:00 p.m. One night, the three of us waited and waited for Max for what seemed like forever. He finally showed up at about ten, in a state of shock. He told us that he had just gone through one of the worst experiences he had ever had as a hotel manager. A guest from New York had arranged to meet his girlfriend at the Palace. He hired a taxi at the Zurich airport to take him to St. Moritz; there was an accident, and he was killed. The girlfriend had arrived earlier, and Max had the terrible burden of giving her the awful news. He then had to call New York and give the same tragic news to the guest's wife.

I continued to play backgammon tournaments at the Palace, where once there was a most unusual occurrence. I had won my first match and walked over to the table where I was slated to play the winner in the next round. A guy and gal were playing. I introduced myself. The guy gave me his name and the gal said, "I'm Joan Palmer." I said, "That's a coincidence! That was my wife's name when I met her!" She asked, "What did you say your name is?"

"Stanley Hirsch." She then pulled her wallet out of her pocketbook and showed me her driver's license. The name on the license was Joan Hirsch. She said, "I was Joan Hirsch before I was Joan Palmer. Your wife was Joan Palmer before she was Joan Hirsch." (This backgammon player became Joan Palmer when she married Jim Palmer, the Hall of Fame pitcher for the Baltimore Orioles.) This was a memorable incident.

St. Moritz is not without many notable incidents. Johannes Badrutt acquired the Pension Faller and renamed it the Hotel Engadiner Kulm. Not only was it the first hotel in St. Moritz at an altitude of 1,856 meters; Badrutt had taken possession of the property in the year 1856. This was the first documented coincidence.

St. Moritz is also the location of many "firsts" in Switzerland. The first electric light was installed at the Kulm Hotel in 1878. The first curling tournament, the first ice skating championships, the first electric tram, the first golf tournament in the Alps, the first ski school, and on and on.

This eminent ski resort proudly points to its selection as host of the Winter Olympics in both 1928 and 1948. Only two other ski centers, Innsbruck in Austria and Lake Placid in New York, share this distinction. For St. Moritz, its inclusion with these other great ski resorts is recognition of its own magnificence and importance in the world of outstanding winter sports.

On a more personal note, the coincidence of the backgammon tournament at the Palace Hotel at the time of Joan's birthday and our introduction to the magnificent snows of St. Moritz has been unforgettable. We have returned time and time again.

SKIING IN ST. MORITZ

Yes, there is skiing in St. Moritz. Well-known as the premier resort of Alpine luxury, it has drawn an international clientele of royalty, celebrities, and aristocrats. This elitist reputation has overshadowed the fact that St. Moritz is actually one of the greatest of all ski resorts because of its fantastic ski terrain and excellent lift system.

Skiing in St. Moritz offers a smorgasbord that appeals to the tastes of skiers of every level, be they beginners, intermediates, advanced, expert, or professional. It is one of only three such resorts that have hosted the Winter Olympics twice, and additionally, it has been the scene of four World Championships.

If you are staying in the heart of St. Moritz, the first lift you will take is a funicular with two sections: the first goes from St. Moritz-Dorf to Chantarella, and the second continues from Chantarella to Corviglia.

In addition to good skiing for beginners, Chantarella also offers some of the most delightful, sun-drenched outdoor restaurants, affordable and not crowded. After lunch, you can pass through Chantarella and ski down to St. Moritz-Dorf to end your day.

The second section of the funicular will bring you to the top station, Corviglia. From there, in just a few steps you will be at a cable car which will take you to the world-renowned peak, Piz Nair, where you will thrill to 360 degrees of astonishing Alpine views. Skiing down from the Piz Nair, a former Olympic run, is primarily for advanced skiers, but with care, it can be negotiated by intermediates. From Corviglia, you have a vast area of intermediate terrain served by several modern quad chairlifts. You can also reach Marguns and the village of Celerina from Corviglia. Marguns also has an array of *al fresco* eating facilities including outdoor bars, a self-service restaurant and a delightful balcony terrace where you will be served delicious Swiss specialties while sunbathing and resting up for afternoon skiing.

An easy afternoon warm-up run will bring you down to Celerina, a typical Italian-style village (although, despite its proximity to Italy, you're still in Switzerland). The runs in Celerina are perfect for beginners taking the next small step to the intermediate level. The lift that will take you back to Marguns is a bubble, or gondola. From Marguns, you have many possibilities to return to Corviglia for the run down to St.Moritz-Dorf, passing through the Chantarella terrain, the last part of which is a long narrow path through the trees. A short walk will bring you into the heart of St. Moritz and a lovely outdoor terrace at the Hotel Hauser where après-skiing begins. If it is too cold, Hanselmann's Tearoom is just a few more steps away. This landmark is a "must" for desserts after skiing.

On the other side of the valley are two huge interconnected areas. The farthest is Furtschellas, which overlooks the village of Sils Maria; the other is Corvatsch, the highest of the St. Moritz peaks, which overlooks Surlej and Lake Silvaplana. Corvatsch also boasts a glacier that accommodates summer skiing. Both areas are served by cable cars leading to terrain with chairlifts and T-bars, with blue and red runs that seem endless. Ski buses, included as part of your lift pass, take you to all of these areas.

There is a ski safari, a guided tour for intermediates and above to introduce newcomers to the terrain on both sides of the valley. From the tourist office in St. Moritz-Dorf, you can join a group, or sign up with the Ski Club of Great Britain which usually participates.

The safari starts with a bus to Sils Maria and a cable car to Furtschellas; this area is commonly known as Sils/Furtschellas. After a few runs accessed by chairlifts, you then ski to Corvatsch, subsequently working your way over to a lift that will bring you to the Hahnensee. This is a fantastic six-mile run to the bottom of the valley. The Hahnensee is rated black but it can be handled by intermediates. About halfway down, you'll stop for lunch on a sunlit terrace. Both the restaurant and the view are exquisite.

At the bottom of the valley, you're on the outskirts of St. Moritz-Bad. With your skis on your shoulder, a few steps will bring you to the Signalbahn, a cable car that will take you to the other side of the valley to the Chantarella/Corviglia/Piz Nair area and then to Marguns and Celerina. Back on the gondola to Marguns, then Corviglia, Chantarella, a traverse through the trees, and you're in St. Moritz-Dorf.

You may not have "earned your wings," but you've certainly earned a drink or dessert at either the Hauser or Hanselmann's. But the pull to return to the areas you've just been introduced to will be strong, since you have only experienced a small part of each.

Our guide for this safari was Nicole Schmidt, a ski instructor from Celerina. As the poster girl for Nivea, the skin-care company, her photos in action on skis and snowboards were everywhere. She sparkled!

After about two weeks, a good skier may be able to do justice to these areas. However, this is not all of the ski terrain available. There's more!

A short ride on a regular (not cog) train, the Rätische Bahn, will take you to Diavolezza. Before skiing here, however, go to the other side of the tracks and you will discover Piz Lagalb. This is a rather small mountain with very big challenges, mainly for advanced and expert skiers since the moguls cover most of the face and, in March, they are tremendous. These bumps cover more than eighty percent of the terrain. The only lift to take is a cable car to the peak. I lucked out the one time I skied it. After a snowfall of about eight inches, we had a beautiful sunny day. The bumps were pillow-soft with all that fresh powder. I skied it with the brother and sister-in-law of Max Keller of the Palace Hotel. Conversation at dinner that night was mainly about fresh powder and bumps—a new kind of "pillow-talk."

Returning to Diavolezza across the railroad tracks, you can see that the face is an intermediate's paradise. However, good skiers don't go to Diavolezza to ski the face. Skiing off-piste from the back starts with a steep bumpy trough with swinging turns from side to side, much like snowboarders do on half-pipes. After about twenty turns, you look down and see where the run meets the Morteratsch Glacier which, like most glaciers, is a flat expanse. Clearly you will need a great deal of momentum to cross as much of the glacier as possible. Even a good schuss off the lower part of the trough won't get you far; you will end up doing a lot of poling, and walking like a cross country skier without the benefit of cross country skis. You may be exhausted, but there is no way out. You can't call a taxi!

You slog on, hoping to get to another slope that goes downhill. Your wishes are ultimately fulfilled, but you are now faced with a different challenge—ice structures such as ridges, precipices, and chasms. And you do something like a slalom to dodge all these hazards. It is dangerously beautiful. If you stop to view these icy structures, tantalizing insights into nature's architecture, you will see sights that are truly astounding. That's the good news. The even better news is that skiing this terrain is not difficult once you take charge of your nerves.

If you were on a cruise ship and crossed the equator, you would receive some sort of certificate. No such citation for crossing the Morteratsch Glacier. Actually you have earned a trophy—the right to tell the story of how you did it! And if you started your day early, you might be able to reward yourself and be served lunch at the Morteratsch restaurant at a different stop on the same railroad line. I once did just that with a ski patroller I met through some good friends at the Palace. (To my surprise, this Swiss patroller, Erica Studer, was also a professional pilot and had once been the personal pilot for the former Shah of Iran.)

Such is the variety and magnificence of St. Moritz skiing, truly a fitting complement to the elegance and glamour of the resort itself. To experience it all requires many visits, which I was fortunate to do because of birthdays, backgammon tournaments, and above all, a special love of skiing.

The author and Miguel on Corviglia, overlooking the lake

**At a rest stop on the Morteratsch Glacier, with the
Ski Club of Great Britain leader and Paul Claeyssens**

BABY STEPS, GIANT STEPS, TRIUMPHS—AND
BROKEN BONES

Who needs ski instruction? Well, if you start skiing at age forty-five, as I did, you do—or a good life insurance policy. Perhaps both.

Through many lessons and exposure to ski schools in Switzerland, France, Austria, and the United States, I acquired a substantial awareness of different skiing techniques. This enabled me to help those who were stronger skiers than I but who were not always in complete control. I seemed to have the ability to spot something that someone else was doing wrong.

One of my appreciative "students" suggested that I take an instructor's class, which I did in Killington, Vermont. On the last day of the week-long class, as an extracurricular bonus, our instructor showed us something he called the "divergent step turn."

How does this differ from an ordinary step or stem turn? Well, instead of stepping on the inside edge of your uphill, or outside, ski you step onto the outside edge of the ski and flip the ski to the inside edge. It's akin to something you do while driving a car: when you want to increase speed, you press down on the accelerator. Switching the pressure from the outside edge to the inside edge is similar. It's a basic racing turn and the acceleration is exhilarating; however, it is somewhat of a paradox. Though you have a very graceful experience completing the turn, the initiation of the turn can be anything but graceful if done at a slow speed.

Before the last skull session of the week, I decided to practice the new turn with a few runs on Snowshed, the beginner's slope. Going up in the chairlift, I mentioned to the fellow sitting next to me (who was not in the class) that I had just learned this terrific turn. He asked if I would show it to him. Once I saw that he wasn't a beginner, I complied. That night, at the bar of the Pickle Barrel, a favorite watering hole, this same fellow tapped me on the shoulder. "Are you the guy who showed me the divergent step turn? I gotta buy you a drink!" It was my first triumph as a ski instructor.

It was not my intention to instruct professionally. All I wanted was to be able to improve my own skills and help others. Call these accomplishments little triumphs or baby steps.

Baby steps? Not always. One of those little triumphs was actually on a slope called Giant Steps in Vail, Colorado. I was skiing with my Brazilian friend Miguel and demonstrating a technique taught to me by Junior Bounous of Snowbird, Utah, for skiing the bumps. The basic idea is to control speed by sideslipping into the mogul and sliding off. That, together with keeping your hands high, enables you to make a very controlled turn. Very rarely do you set an edge, for that will speed you up.

In the instructors' class, the basic admonition is "terrain, terrain, terrain—don't instruct on difficult terrain!" I ignored the admonition, since Giant Steps, as you might guess, had huge bumps. After a few moguls, my most educable friend Miguel picked up the technique handily. The next very steep slope, Pepi's Face, leads down to the center of Vail, and we celebrated Miguel's satisfying accomplishment at Pepi's own Gasthof Gramshammer. Lunch on the sun-drenched terrace at Pepi's is a delightful way to enjoy another little triumph, another baby step.

So what happened the next time we came down Giant Steps? I skied down a few bumps, stopped and turned to watch Miguel. Oops, my mistake! I lost my edge, fell backward, my pole jammed into my side, and I wound up with a broken rib. Making it back to Pepi's was painful, but Pepi's Sacher Torte, broken rib notwithstanding, was worth it.

That was only the second broken bone I experienced in my seventy-eight years. The first occurred while skiing in Zermatt the year before.

In Zermatt, at the bottom of National, a black run from Blauherd to Sunnega, is a quad chair. As you come down National, the lift is straight ahead, and there's no problem reaching it. If you choose to take the easier run from the Sunnega station of the funicular, arrival at the turnstiles to board the lift requires a turn of about 150 degrees around the netting which protects you from falling into a chasm. Careful skiers make that turn very slowly.

Sometimes, however, stupidity reigns supreme. Back-marking for the Ski Club of Great Britain (ensuring that the group stayed together and got down safely), I was distracted by someone on the chairlift and wound up wrestling with the netting. (I might have preferred to have wrestled with that someone who distracted me!) I thought I had merely sprained my wrist and continued skiing, but when we reached Furgg on the Trockener Steg side, the pain got to me. I decided to stop at a restaurant and sat outside applying snow to my hand and wrist.

The man sitting next to me, who turned out to be a physician from Holland, asked what had happened and began to examine my hand and wrist. I said that I didn't think anything was broken because I could move my fingers, but he said that wasn't necessarily so. He gave me some pills for the pain and suggested I have my hand X-rayed. "Later," I said, "now let's ski."

I made some runs with him and his wife, and we wound up skiing together the rest of the week, as I consumed his inventory of pain pills. I gave a lesson to his sister-in-law, a new skier, and we finished the week at the cafe on Riffelalp, outside this newly built beautiful five-star hotel. He examined my hand again, and because the swelling had not gone down, he made me promise to see a doctor when I got home.

I kept my promise. I had a broken fifth metacarpal, the bone leading to the pinky on my right hand. It was the first fracture I had had in my seventy-seven years! I was in a splint for about four weeks and was so happy that I had not had it X-rayed when my Dutch doctor first suggested it. With my hand in a splint I would have missed an entire week of skiing.

When I arrived home, I had a very sweet note from the doctor's sister-in-law telling me how much she appreciated the lesson. Another small triumph, another baby step.

Yes, this was my first fracture, and as you can surmise, injuries and triumphs seem to go hand in hand.

A trip to Verbier one Christmas holiday started with very poor ski conditions which worsened as the New Year arrived. I had heard that the snow in Zermatt was better, so off I went. The snow wasn't much better, but I hooked up with a group from the Ski Club of Great Britain.

Skiing down from the top of Gornergrat, the Ski Club leader assigned me to back-mark. The night before we had a snowfall of about four inches so I decided to venture off the groomed piste. Another example of supreme stupidity: I hit a rock, both skis released, and I was vaulted head first into another rock. (As I recounted this mishap later, I said I hit a rock, and it hit me back.)

I was knocked out for a moment, and when I came to, a doctor from Boston and his daughter, an emergency medical technician, were hovering over me, applying snow to my head to slow the bleeding. Soon the ski patrol arrived with a toboggan, but I insisted that I was able to ski. The patrol followed me down to Riffelberg where I finally succumbed to their demands and took the Gornergratbahn down to Zermatt and a doctor's office. I had a gash in my head that required five stitches to close, which I was instructed to have removed in a week. The bill from the doctor made an even larger gash in my wallet.

After a few days of scratchy snow in Zermatt, I decided to relocate to Courchevel, as there were reports of good snow in Les Trois Vallées in France, a vast interconnected area with two hundred ski lifts. It encompasses four levels of Courchevel, Meribel, Mottaret, Les Menuires, St. Martin de Belleville, and Val Thorens.

Coming up on the Verdons bubble, or gondola, the two Englishmen in the car asked me what had happened to my head. I told them and said that it was now a week and I hoped that removing the stitches was not going to be as costly as getting them. They laughed and told me that they were surgeons with the Royal Navy, and if I met them with a pair of scissors on La Croisette, it would only cost me a few beers. After skiing down with them, I went to my hotel and got the scissors. Removing the stitches took just a few minutes. Downing the beers took a good deal longer.

Realizing that they were relatively new skiers, I told them that I was an instructor and offered to help them. We spent the following morning together, and when I returned to my hotel that afternoon, there was a bottle of champagne with a note saying it was the best ski lesson they had ever had. What a triumph! A giant step! You can't imagine how quickly my wound healed without a trace of a scar.

Some of the techniques I "learned" were self-taught or self-discovered. I skied one week in Aspen with Inge Lesjak, a lovely lady who is an expert on skiing in Slovenia. She named one of these techniques the *Stanley Turn*. It is best described in a letter she wrote:

> *I would like to say that one of your "ski better tips" helped me to improve my skiing by far. In Aspen a couple of years ago, I was impressed how you conquered some of the steeper hills (especially with metal hips and breathing hard) and you told me the trick is to keep your hands in front and close to your chest and then execute turns by planting your poles downhill left and right. It makes me ski more controlled. Whatever the correct term is for this style, I call it the Stanley Turn. Whenever I feel I pick up too much speed I quickly remember to do a "Stanley" and I feel fine.*

Thanks, Inge . . . I would only add that the pole plant should not be near the shovel of the ski but alongside the boot.

Another technique was named the *Hirsch Glance* by a Scot skiing in Aspen with the Ski Club of Great Britain. (Yes, this club has leaders in Aspen and Vail.) A parallel turn has become simplified because of the parabolic curvature of the new "shaped" skis. All that is needed is a shift of weight to the uphill, or outside, ski and, because of the ski's curvature, the turn is automatic. A shift to the right ski makes the left turn and vice versa. A very easy way to shift your weight in this manner is a quick glance uphill at the top, or initiation, of the turn for just a split second. Your weight will automatically shift to the uphill ski.

It's just a glance, for your eyes should return *immediately* to looking downhill. Try it on dry land without skis. Stand with your feet shoulder-width apart, arms outstretched in front of you, and glance to the left. Your weight should shift to your left leg without any other conscious movement on your part. While skiing, it's very important to remember that it's just a glance; your eyes and head should return immediately to looking downhill. That's the Hirsch Glance.

It is said that all things good or bad come in threes, and yes, I did have a third fracture, but I'll take that up in another chapter.

ITALY, AUSTRIA, FAVORITES,
AND A CIRCUS

Alabaster from Volterra, Venetian glass from Murano, majolica from Montelupo, and wrought iron from Firenze. These were my favorite things: artware our family business imported from Italy.

Lamps and giftware were an integral part of the J. B. Hirsch Company, our family business established in 1907 by my grandfather, Joseph. I represented the third generation. An annual buying trip to Europe afforded me many trips to Italy, France, Spain, Germany, Czechoslovakia, and Austria.

For Easter in April 1973, I decided to combine a three-week buying trip to Italy, from where we imported most of our items, with a family ski vacation. It would be the first of many trips combining business and skiing. Of course, it had to be planned to coordinate with the school holiday.

My parents were in New York when I told them of my plans to finish my buying trip in northern Italy and then drive to Lech in the Arlberg region of Austria, and meet there with Joan and the boys.

My father, Abe, was as successful in his field as his brother Jack (Burnet Hershey) was in his. After WW II, Dad was a pioneer in the industry for the importing of majolica, alabaster, and Venetian glass from Italy. He turned the J.B. Hirsch foundry into one of the leading lamp manufacturers in the United States. Before retiring in the early '60s, he trained me to take his place in the family business.

Listening to my plans for the forthcoming trip, he said, "I haven't been to Italy in over ten years. Oh, would I love to go." My mother, in a rare, gracious moment, said "Abe, you want to go? GO!" Without a pause, he directed my travel agent wife, "Joan, book me!"

We went to Italy together. It was a great treat to be with him for three weeks after so many years since our last trip together.

The reception Dad received at the various factories we visited was remarkable. So many owners greeted him with profound expressions of gratitude for what he had done to open up the American market for their wares.

Dad had a wonderful sense of humor and an uncanny ability to communicate even with those whose language he didn't speak. His greatest pleasure was to have others laugh with him. He related well to the owners' families, especially the children, for he knew how to play and laugh with them. The children weren't shy in showing how fond they were of him. It was so enriching for me that others felt the same about him as I did. He always left behind such warm memories.

We worked our way up from south to north in the boot of Italy, from Naples to Rome to Florence, then Venice and Vicenza. But we were mostly in small villages such as Deruta, Montelupo, Volterra, Empoli, and Nove, the homes of the artisans. We finished in Bassano del Grappa, renowned for its ceramics and, of course, the liqueur Grappa, Italy's "liquid fire."

In Vicenza, we rented a Fiat 124. We said *arrivedérci* to our *commissionaire* and headed north to Austria. The three-week buying trip in Italy was over. It probably could have been done in two weeks if not for the drinking, card tricks, and laughing with the families, but it wouldn't have been as enjoyable.

Austria has some of the best Alpine ski areas and regions. The region of the Zillertal Valley contains Gerlos, Fügen, Finkenberg, Hintertux and Mayrhofen. Within one hour of Salzburg, there are Ellmau, Dorfgastein, Schladming, St. Johann, and forty more ski areas. An hour and a half away are Kitzbühel, Badgastein, Zell am See, Kaprun, Saalbach/Hinterglemm, and forty-five more. Near Innsbruck are Igls, the Stubai Glacier, Seefeld, Alpbach, Ischgl (which connects to Samnaun in Switzerland), and countless others. However, a poll of experts has crowned the Arlberg region as not only the best in Austria but one of the best in the world. I heartily agree.

Driving north from Bassano del Grappa, we went past Bolzano, a world-renowned wood carving region, and took the Brenner Pass, the principal Alpine pass between Italy and Austria. It started snowing heavily as we approached St. Anton, where we stopped for dinner.

Separating the two sections of the Arlberg is the Arlberg Pass, once a treacherous route which travelers avoided for centuries, opting instead for the Fern Pass, although it was more roundabout. Now, however, as an assist to the skiing industry, a more modern road has been built on the Arlberg Pass.

The principal ski area in the southern sector is St. Anton. The principal ski areas in the other sector are Lech, Zürs, and Zug am Arlberg. Lech was our destination, and the only way to get there was over the Arlberg Pass.

The snow kept falling heavily. When we finished dinner, we were told that we had better put on chains to get over the pass. Since we didn't have chains, we would have to overnight in St. Anton in order to buy a set in the morning.

Dad said, "Come on! We have a new car with new tires, we'll make it." At seventy-five, his spirit for adventure was as strong as ever.

As we drove up the unplowed road, I was afraid that if I stopped, I wouldn't have enough traction to get going again. I kept in low gear and held my foot on the accelerator very gingerly. I had just had my forty-sixth birthday and began to wonder if I would make it to my forty-seventh.

After more than a few harrowing moments with our wheels spinning in the snow, we finally made it to the top. From there, I kept my foot off the accelerator, letting gravity take us to Lech. It was still treacherous, with occasional skidding, but we made it. Fortunately, Haus Lech, our hotel, was immediately on the right. Things were looking up.

When I sat down in our room, my hands were trembling. "Why are you shaking like that?"

"Dad, I wasn't sure we were going to make it up that hill, and I didn't know what I would do if we ever stopped."

"Nonsense, I knew you would have no problem."

"No problem? Of course not."

The following year, work on the Arlberg Road Tunnel was begun and it was completed in December 1978. Now there really is "no problem."

The next day was beautiful, with not a cloud in the sky. We took the cable car up to Oberlech where the Burg Hotel had a nice deck. Dad was very comfortable sitting there in the sun, reading *The International Herald Tribune.*

I got into my skis and took a lift to the top. The snow was marvelous and well-groomed. Being a new skier with not much experience in fresh powder, I stayed on the groomed slopes, but I booked a powder lesson for the next day. It helped a great deal, but if I got into snow that was over my ankles, handling it was "over my head."

The rest of the family arrived the following day, and we enrolled the boys in ski school. They were reluctant, confident that since they had taken lessons in Zermatt during the Christmas holidays, they didn't need any more. In addition, it was more important to spend more time with grandpa!

The weather was wonderful. Joan and I enjoyed the sun and the easy skiing, but we also took half-day lessons. We met Dad for lunch on the deck of the hotel. He said, "Next time you come to Lech, why don't you stay here? You walk out the door, put on your skis, and you're skiing." It was a great suggestion, and we booked the Burg Hotel for that Christmas.

At dinner that night, he made a surprise announcement. "You know that I left Romania in 1900 when I was two years old, and I have never been back. I just contacted my mother's family, and tomorrow I'm taking the bus back to Zurich and flying to Bucharest. The Bughici family will meet me at the airport." Off he went the next day to meet his family.

**Abe Hirsch, the author's father, the first skier in the family
on a buying trip to Czechoslovakia in 1929**

For the rest of the holiday, we continued to take lessons. The boys had graduated to a class with adult skiers, and Jamie shared the honor of being at the top of the class with a sixty-five-year-old gentleman from Australia who had come to Austria to learn to ski.

When we finished this lovely Easter holiday, Joan and the boys went home while I headed back to Italy to attend the Milan Fair, stopping in St.

Moritz for two days. It was my first time skiing in that great resort, but I've been back more than a dozen times since.

Before my folks went back to Florida, we all met for dinner at my sister's home, and Dad told at great length of his meeting with the Bughici family. He finished by pulling out a large cardboard chart, the Bughici family tree, where Jamie's and Michael's names were the last to be entered.

We returned to Lech for Christmas 1973. The Burg Hotel is situated at the top station of the cable car, making it easy to get down to the village and is within a few turns to lifts that go higher and give access to the entire area.

Lech is interconnected to the plush resort of Zürs and Zug am Arlberg, a small, charming village. Skiing from Oberlech to Lech to Zürs to Zug is known as a *circus*, the last part of the roundabout that brings you back to Oberlech. The historic name of this circus is the White Ring, and it is a popular three-hour tour for strong intermediates. It's a great run on the Madloch side of the valley, with the chairlift bringing you up to the 7,997-foot Madloch Joch.

On the other side of the Arlberg is St. Anton, the most popular area of the region, with many challenging black runs and blue and red intermediate runs as well. It is connected to two areas, mainly intermediate, St. Christoph and St. Jakob. There are no groomed runs that interconnect with any part of the Lech/Zürs/Zug Circus but, with a guide, experts can climb to the top of the Valluga (the highest mountain in the Arlberg) and ski off-piste down to Zürs. The rainbow of runs, green, blue, red, and black in St. Anton serves all abilities, but its après-ski nightlife is just as responsible for its popularity.

I have skied more areas in Austria than in any other country in the Alps. Undoubtedly, the Arlberg is my favorite. So what is my favorite in Italy? It is Cortina d'Ampezzo.

Cortina has a ranking comparable to that of the Arlberg, a skiing region with a great variety of areas. In the northeast corner of Italy, it is surrounded by the Enchanted Kingdom, the Dolomites. This immense mountain range has a fantastic history going back 270 million years when it was formed by the movement of tectonic plates. The Dolomite Road offers one of the most scenic drives in all the world, stretching from Cortina in the east to Bolzano in the west.

Cortina skiing is the crown jewel of the Dolomites. The area hosted the 1956 Winter Olympics. Among the many films made there is the James

Bond thriller, *For Your Eyes Only*, with its memorable stunt sequences filmed on Cortina's slopes.

Miguel and his wife, Gisele, with the author in Cortina

One of the many joys recently has been skiing with my son Michael (who now lives in Bangkok) together with my Brazilian friend Miguel. I met Miguel in 1999 in St. Moritz, and in the years since, we have become so close that I think of him and his wife, Gisele, as family. We have skied together every year since 1999. Though thousands of miles separate Michael, Miguel, and me, I couldn't feel closer to each of them: Michael, of course, and the friendship with Miguel continues to grow.

Miguel and I have an ongoing contest. He's trying to make me a wine lover and I'm trying to make him a ski bum. His knowledge of and taste in wines are astonishing, especially to this former beer drinker. I think he's winning.

One day in Cortina, we stopped for lunch in a small valley at the foot of one of the lifts. We were seated at a table with about eight others, and the conversation was international and quite boisterous. Michael is fluent in French, Miguel in Italian, Spanish, and, of course, Portuguese. I managed to exercise my German, but, actually, we all spoke English.

The stories and banter went back and forth. We three told of individual amusing incidents and also of things that happened when we skied together.

Soon, we were surrounded by a group of about fifteen; we actually had an audience! (Over the years, Miguel's version has expanded the audience to more than fifty!)

Mindful of the warning not to mix business with pleasure, I decided to turn the family business over to my nephew, Jeffrey. Now it was in the hands of the fourth generation, leaving me free to devote more time to skiing. That decision obviously was the right one for me!

Michael in Davos supporting the former First Lady

EQUIPMENT

ADVANCES AND ADVENTURES

Prior to the twentieth century, all skis were made of wood. Hickory skis, introduced in 1911, were the standard until 1933 when the first laminated skis were developed.

Just a year later, in 1934, aluminum skis appeared in France, and in 1960, fiberglass skis came on the market.

The first cable binding, allowing a skier's heel to be held securely to the ski, was developed in 1935. Known as the Kandahar, it's a name that permeates the ski world now for the names of races, places, hotels, and what-not. A few years after the Kandahar's introduction, a successful release binding was introduced, permitting the ski to fall away from the skier who has fallen. Leg fractures became much rarer on the slopes.

Buckle boots arrived in 1955, and leather boots were on their way out. All-plastic boots, which keep the skier's foot stationary, were introduced in 1964. Skiers now had complete control of their skis, no longer at the mercy of leather and other flexible materials.

These developments pale compared to those introduced since I started to ski in 1972. Since then, improvements have been remarkable for all the major components: skis, boots, bindings and poles have all undergone great advances. (These pages will not deal with other, less elementary, components such as gloves, goggles, and helmets, all of which have also been improved greatly.)

BOOTS

Probably the leather boots I originally skied in were the last of their generation. It took a bit of time and a lot of strength to lace them up, but they were extremely comfortable and flexible. However, softness and flexibility turned out to be the very qualities that advanced skiers did not want. Strong control of the skis requires that a skier's feet be in rigid containers; plastic ski boots with adjustable buckles instead of laces have proved to be the answer.

For those of us with arthritis in our hips, reaching down to the buckles to snap them in place requires a certain "key" to get the necessary leverage. Adjusting the buckles so that there would be little or no movement of the foot in the boot necessitates lifting and closing of the buckles several times. The key is essential and is somewhat like an ordinary bottle opener.

Then Salomon, a manufacturer, introduced the rear-entry boot. What a blessing to those arthritics among us! The boots were easily slipped into and the single, reachable, adjustable buckle in the rear clamped the foot firmly in the boot with just one press of the hand.

My rear-entry boots finally wore out after years of wear. The heel gave way and could neither be repaired nor replaced. I was in Vail and went to Surefoot, one of the largest chains of ski boot retailers. "Sorry, rear-entry boots are no longer made. The industry has determined that the overlap boot (front-entry) gives much more control," I was told. (I couldn't disagree more with that assessment.)

So I tried about fifteen overlap boots and, because of my oddly shaped feet, not one fit. Then I tried one that was labeled "soft." I skied in them for half a day, but they needed constant adjustments. I could not adjust the buckles without getting out of my skis in order to sit down to reach them. I took them back and sat in the shop as the helpful staff called all over Colorado to try to locate a pair of rear-entry boots. I was impressed with the effort that Surefoot exercised to find a boot for me, but they were not successful.

A young man sat down next to me and asked what my problem was. He asked my boot size and then told me that his dad had stopped skiing and had a pair of rear-entry boots, used just a few times, that might fit me. We met the following morning; I tried the boots on and was delirious. They fit! I asked how much he wanted for them, and when he said "$50," I said, "WHAT? They look brand new; they must be worth at least $100." We compromised at $75. I would have happily paid him ten or twenty times that price. I had thought that if I couldn't find a pair of rear-entry boots to fit me, my skiing days would be over.

But if you ever need someone to negotiate a price for you, I am obviously not a good choice.

SKI POLES

The improvements in ski poles have not been particularly remarkable, but interestingly, two of them have resulted in my losing my poles. One incident was a temporary loss, the other was permanent.

Most ski poles have pistol grips with indentations for your fingers, allowing for a more secure hold. They also have a strap that fits around the wrist, although it is safer not to put your hands through the straps.

In the 1970s, Scott produced a pole with an extreme pistol grip that encircled the hand. Instead of a strap there was about a one-inch opening in the grip that enabled you to hang the poles on the safety bar of a chairlift. This freed your hands so that you could sit on them, reach into your pockets, or embrace your partner. Not having straps was another advantage for safety reasons—and eliminated the nuisance of having to remove them when boarding a chairlift.

In a rare moment of generosity, my friend Abe was so taken with this vast improvement that he presented me with a pair of these new poles on a trip to Stowe, Vermont.

The first chairlift at Stowe rode above National, a very steep narrow trail that went straight down the fall line. Abe showed me how convenient it was to hang these new poles on the safety bar. He neglected to point out that the open part of the grip should be facing outward, not facing me, for if the opening was facing me and I leaned forward, I would knock the poles off the safety bar—and, of course, that's exactly what happened. I leaned forward, and the ski poles fell on National. Since we were relatively new skiers, retrieving the poles on this very difficult slope was nearly a National disaster.

Of course, without poles, I was unable to ski down National to retrieve them. Abe, eleven years my junior, gallantly volunteered to perform the rescue. He nearly killed himself but arrived in one piece at the bottom of the lift, holding two pairs of these "fantastic" ski poles. He did this in less than two hours. His generosity in presenting me with these new poles was greatly appreciated, but it was proof of the adage, "No good deed goes unpunished."

Years later, titanium ski poles were developed. These ultralight, nearly pencil-thin poles were both desirable and very expensive. An appreciative young woman in Telluride to whom I had given some instruction presented me with a pair. It was a gift I couldn't graciously refuse. However, if I am ever offered such a gift again, I will, yes, I will refuse it. These poles were so desirable that they were stolen from me in, of all places, the poshest of ski areas, Deer Valley.

I now ski with a pair of slightly bent, very old ski poles I obtained in a rental shop for $10. I have refused all offers by ski shops to straighten them out. Those slight bends are my assurance that they will never be stolen. No one wants these ugly things. I've had them for years.

SKIS

Call them shaped, parabolic, extreme side-cut, or whatever, they are the most important advance in ski design since I took up the sport.

Shaped skis are wide at the tip (shovel), thin at the waist, and wide at the tail. The extra surface allows for skiing on shorter skis with as much stability as on longer skis. I am now skiing on 160 cm skis when just a few years ago I was skiing on 200 cm skis.

They are ultramaneuverable, and unweighting to make a parallel turn is a thing of the past. A simple shift of weight to the uphill or outside ski and the turn is almost automatic. Of course, you can still unweight to make the turn, and probably, the combination of shifting and simultaneous unweighting is how most turns are made on shaped skis. However, in powder, unweighting is the dominant technique for making the turn.

The author in Valle Nevado, Chile, on 200 cm skis

My all-mountain shaped skis are good on groomed slopes, bumps, and powder. What more could a geriatric ski bum ask for? Perhaps they will help me reach my goal of continuing to ski when I am ninety-three years old.

I often ride a chairlift with someone who is decades younger than I am. When I tell him that I ski only GS, he says, incredulously, "You do Giant Slalom?" I reply, "No, I do Geriatric Skiing."

BINDINGS, BRAKES, AND BURT

Runaway skis can be deadly. They become uncontrolled missiles that can maim or kill innocent skiers or bystanders. Therefore, all ski bindings today have brakes, prongs that descend to grab the snow when skis are released from the boots at the time of impact during a fall. The prongs prevent the skis from sliding and becoming deadly missiles.

The ski binding is the contraption that attaches the boot to the ski. Prior to ski brakes, bindings had safety straps that encircled the boot, preventing the ski from running away. Very rarely would the force of a wipe-out break a safety strap. However, too often the released ski would behave like a windmill and injure the skier, because the ski was still attached. Ski brakes solved the problem, allowing the released ski to fall away from the skier. No more windmill injuries.

At about the same time that ski brakes were introduced, a fellow by the name of Burt Weinstein developed a unique plate binding called the Burt Binding, featuring two spring-loaded retractable cables in the front and back of each binding. In the event of a fall whose impact causes the ski to disconnect from the binding, the ski snaps back into place automatically by just a slight movement. This takes the pressure off the cables, allowing them to spring back to their original position, which can be done by simply raising a leg; there is nothing more that the skier needs to do. No resetting the back of the binding, no cleaning snow off the binding, no digging skis out from deep snow or removing a safety strap and then tying it back on, and no replacing the boot into the binding. All the skier has to do is get up and ski.

What a gift to a skier like me with arthritic hips!!

The only time that the spring cables might break is when the force of the impact is as great as that which would break a safety strap. Fortunately, a rare possibility.

I was delighted to ski with these Burt Bindings for the first time at Snowbird, Utah, which had opened in December 1971, just two years before. Skiing down on Election, a blue run, I hit a bump hard, got some air, felt the binding release—but in a mini-second, the ski snapped back to my boot and I continued skiing. It was miraculous. With any other binding I would have been sprawled in the snow. What a bonanza!

Just as I made a turn at the bottom of Election I saw five skiers, all wearing Burt Bindings. I stopped to talk with one of them, a good-looking guy in an all-yellow ski suit. I was exulting about this experience I had just had. He invited me to join their group, and we skied down to the Gad II chairlift together. When we got on the lift he introduced himself. "My name is Dick Bass. What's yours?"

Well! Dick Bass, the developer and owner of Snowbird, took me to places on that mountain that I have never been able to find again. It was an inspirational experience for me. Twelve years later, on April 30,1985, Bass became the first man to complete the challenge of climbing to the highest point on each of the seven continents: Denali (Mt. McKinley), North America; Aconcagua, South America; Mt. Elbrus, Europe; Mount Kilimanjaro, Africa; Vinson, Antarctica; Mt. Kosciusko, Australia; and Mt. Everest, Asia. He also held the record of being the oldest person ever to have climbed Mt. Everest. He is two years younger than I. If he had asked me to join him then, as he did at Snowbird, would I be the one to hold that record? (His incredible climbing adventures are vividly described in the book *Seven Summits*.)

The next Thanksgiving weekend, following a business event in Denver, I visited a friend in Aspen. It snowed and snowed. Skiing in Aspen Highlands in all that powder was a real treat for an Eastern skier, and it was only November. I got adventurous and went off-piste, where there were no groomed slopes, and into the trees. *Big mistake!* My ski tips dipped into a depression and that very rare, almost impossible thing, happened. All four cables on the Burt Bindings broke. I did a somersault, landing on my butt. My skis ran away. My friend retrieved my skis but there was no way I could get them back on. I tried to remove the plates from the bottom of my boots so I could walk down but I couldn't. Fortunately, the bottoms of the plates were highly polished. Yes, they were skiable! Probably the shortest skis anyone ever skied on.

There was not enough snow at the bottom of Aspen Highlands to ski down to the base. Everyone was downlifting on the bottom chairlift. When I approached the lift, those on this long line waiting for the chairlift were incredulous. "Where are your skis?" I replied, "Like the economy, I lost them in a depression."

SENIOR MOMENTS

The term "senior moment" usually refers to a lapse in memory by an elderly person and the consequences of these short-term lapses. However, there are moments that have affected seniors on the younger side of elderly that do not necessarily involve memory.

There are incidents when a senior's attention might be directed toward something quite minor. This might serve to distract him from the major thing he is doing, causing him to wind up in a place he doesn't want to be. Call these incidents *mindless* senior moments.

There are times when it finally dawns upon a senior that he no longer has that younger appearance. This can be a *crushing* senior moment.

There are also episodes in the life of a senior when his unthinking carelessness endangers him and others. These are truly *irresponsible* senior moments.

The episodes to follow illustrate my own, often abashed, involvement in some of these moments.

THE BUS

As a family, we celebrated seventeen Christmas and New Year holidays in Val d'Isère. We stayed at the Chamois d'Or, a charming chalet-style hotel at the base of Bellevarde, the site of the giant slalom and downhill runs during the 1992 Winter Olympics. The proprietors were Jacques and Jackie LaBorde, and after seventeen years, we were like family.

We would fly to Geneva, and if we avoided the weekend, the bus to Val d'Isère was not crowded, at times almost empty. On this particular trip, we arrived in Geneva on Friday, and when we boarded the bus, it was just Joan and me, our two sons, Jamie and Michael, another couple, and a very attractive young woman. Our boys, thirteen and fourteen, sat in the rear, the other couple a few rows before them, the two of us about the fifth row, and across the aisle was this young woman who was more than just attractive.

When the bus would stop in Moutiers, those going to Courchevel or any of the other resorts in Les Trois Vallées would transfer to another bus. The only person on our bus to make this transfer was the lovely young woman. The stop was also a railroad station, and I would always get off the bus to take advantage of the facilities and to get a cup of coffee; there was usually enough time to do this while luggage was being unloaded and transferred. However, this time, since there was only one person making the transfer, it took only a moment. When I returned to the bus, it was not there. It had left, and I was left with only a shirt and sweater on my back and a wallet that was just about empty.

I grabbed a taxi. The driver assured me that we would catch the bus at Bourg St. Maurice, the next station about half an hour away, just before the long climb to Tignes and Val d'Isère. No such luck! Most of the way, we were stuck behind a slow-moving truck, and when we finally reached Bourg St. Maurice, the bus had already gone. I had to take the taxi all the rest of the way.

The bus traveled a more circuitous route, going first to Tignes before arriving in Val d'Isère, so I got to the Chamois d'Or ahead of Joan and the boys. Getting the money for the taxi from Jacques and then trying to explain why I had no luggage and where the rest of the family was took a little time. Shortly thereafter, the family arrived.

I was more than just a little cross, but Joan explained that she had fallen asleep and didn't awaken until after the bus had left Bourg St. Maurice. The boys said they saw me get off the bus, and when I didn't get back on, they assumed I was on my way to Courchevel with Cheryl Tieg. That young woman was the supermodel Cheryl Tieg? If I had known that, perhaps I wouldn't have made it to Val d'Isère at all!

A senior moment? More like a senior fantasy!

WHAT A DIFFERENCE
A YEAR MAKES!

Since I started skiing, I've had a special addiction to spring skiing and, to celebrate my birthday in April, I've managed to ski at that time every year. Most of those trips have been to Utah where I once had a condo at the Canyon Racquet Club.

At one time, Snowbird (where conditions in the spring have generally been the best) treated seniors sixty-two years and over to the same lift ticket price as children. Twenty-two years ago, I turned sixty-two on April 8. I went to the ticket window and requested a senior ticket. The woman behind the counter looked up at me and asked for proof of age. Having left my driver's license and wallet at the condo, I naturally didn't have such proof with me. It was quite a hassle, but I was finally successful in getting the ticket with the admonition that I had better have proof of age next time!

The following year, I made sure my wallet and driver's license were with me when I requested a senior lift ticket. As the clerk started to process my request, I asked, "Don't you want proof of age?" She looked up at me and said "No, that's not necessary."

You can imagine my dismay. Now came the realization that yes, I am a senior. It was a senior moment that is difficult to forget—even to this day! I was crushed.

WHO'S WITH YOU?

When conditions are right in the Tarentaise section of the Haute-Savoie in France, the École du Ski Français has a tour for Class One skiers, offered just once a week, from Val d'Isère/ Tignes off-piste through the valley to La Plagne.

I arrived at this ski school's office just a few minutes after the group had left, too late to register for the tour. However, the clerk told me that the group would be taking the bus to La Daille, the telecabine to the midstation, the Tommeuse lift to Tovière and then ski down to Val Claret in Tignes to take the Poma lift to the Col du Pâlet. From the top of the Col du Pâlet they would ski out of the area, through the valley to La Plagne. Of course, it would be all off-piste skiing in fresh snow until they would get to La Plagne.

I knew the route to the Col du Pâlet quite well, and since they were a group of twelve, I thought it wouldn't be difficult to catch up with them. *I was wrong!* I didn't realize that, because they were with a guide from the ski school, they would have priority on the lift lines. Nevertheless, when I got to the Col du Pâlet Poma lift, I saw them unloading at the top and figured that I was not too far behind. *Wrong again!* They had climbed about seventy-five yards to the top of the Col du Pâlet, from which they would go out of bounds (off-piste) through fresh powder through the valley to La Plagne.

Once they got off the lift and climbed to the top of the Col du Pâlet, their tracks in the fresh snow were quite discernible. I figured that I could follow their tracks and eventually catch up. *Wrong again*—but now I got lucky. One in the group had lost the basket of his ski pole and was trekking back to get it, holding his fellow skiers up for a few minutes. I had finally caught up with them.

When the guide saw me, he began to argue vehemently with an Englishwoman in the group. I asked her why he was yelling at her, and she said, "He's not yelling at me, he's yelling at you. He wants to know *who is with you?*" When I told her I was alone, she said, "That's why he's yelling. There will be no one past this point for a week. If you had fallen, broken a binding, or had any mishaps at all, your body probably wouldn't be found until the spring." I shuddered.

The guide put me second in the line behind him. As we were traversing across the bank of the valley, the snow broke and a small avalanche carried him and the skier ahead of me down about thirty yards. I had stopped just about a foot from the break. The guide and the skier were buried up to their hips, but after a good deal of digging, they extricated themselves, retrieved their skis, and we were on our way. With that event in mind, I asked the guide about the danger of the tour. He said there wasn't that much snow in December, but later in the season, after greater snowfalls, it would be too dangerous to make the tour at all.

We finally reached La Plagne and were treated to a well-earned feast of chacroute for lunch. We finished the day skiing on the groomed pistes of La Plagne, which was a treat for our legs after having gone through such heavy powder. It took about an hour by taxi to get back to Val d'Isère.

When I went to sleep that night, I had more than a moment to realize how *stupid* I had been; not only was I skiing alone, but since I hadn't registered for the tour, no one would have known my whereabouts. It could have been a disastrous mistake, a mindless senior moment. How lucky I was!

RESPONSIBILITIES AND
THEIR ABSENCE

On December 31, 1997, Michael Kennedy, son of the former senator and presidential candidate Robert Kennedy, was playing touch football, a sport the Kennedy clan regularly played on the family campground lawn in Hyannisport on Cape Cod.

However, on this day, the game wasn't being played on the grounds of the Kennedy compound, but on the ski slopes of Aspen, Colorado, and all the players were on skis. Kennedy, in an attempt to catch the football, lost control and slammed into a tree. The crash was fatal. Although first aid was administered by the ski patrol, it was to no avail. He was taken to the hospital where he was pronounced dead. It was still another of the countless tragedies that have plagued the Kennedy family over the years.

Less than a week later, on January 6, 1998, U.S. Congressman (and former half of the famed duo Sonny and Cher) Sonny Bono was reported missing at Heavenly Valley Ski Area in South Lake Tahoe, California. He was found two hours later by the ski patrol on the Nevada side of the mountain. They reported that he had been on the Orion slope, and after skiing beneath a chairlift, he hit a tree. He was skiing alone; no one knows any other details of the accident or how he died. *He was skiing alone!*

There are two things that responsible skiers will tell you about both of these terrible events: First, do not *deliberately* do anything on skis that will cause you to lose control. Second, *do not ski alone!* The first is a responsibility you have to yourself as well as to other skiers. The second is a responsibility you have to yourself and your family.

In the same month as Bono's accident, I was skiing with the Ski Club of Great Britain in Val d'Isère. After a few days of sunny weather, the club leader announced that a heavy snowfall was expected the next day, and there would be a whiteout if we skied above the tree line. Whiteouts in the Alps, where most of the skiing is above the tree line, are not a great deal of fun. The white snow and white clouded sky join together to form a wall of white. As in a blackout, you have no visibility. However, trees in a whiteout can be likened to candles in a blackout: they help you to see. Candles provide illumination in a blackout; trees provide contrast in a whiteout. Skiing in a whiteout requires an extra measure of control even though your legs have to be relaxed in order to absorb the unseen bumps and other changes in terrain. It is also your responsibility to maintain extra distance from other skiers to avoid collisions—no tailgating!

When the ski club leader said that we would ski in the trees the next day in order to avoid the whiteout, bearing in mind what had happened to Michael Kennedy and Sonny Bono made me hesitate to join the group. I didn't consider that "skiing in the trees" can have two different meanings.

The first refers to slopes that are not groomed and have trees scattered randomly; these are called gladed areas. Because a great deal of skill is required in order to avoid hitting a tree, these slopes should be skied only by advanced and expert skiers. The second refers to groomed slopes bordered by trees on each side. These can be quite comfortable and therefore handled easily by intermediate skiers. On reflection, I realized that it was the latter that the leader meant.

The expected heavy snowfall ended early in the morning, and we joyously skied powder in the sunshine. As with most skiing in the Alps, we skied above the tree line.

Controlled skiing is every skier's responsibility, but I doubt if there has ever been a skier who has never lost control. There have been many deaths and injuries caused by skiers out of control, but the cause has not always been one of irresponsibility. There are many reasons for loss of control, including unseen obstacles such as rocks, branches and roots, as well as conditions such as whiteouts, snow slides, and overcrowded slopes.

Ice and hard-pack are major hazards. Yes, there is a difference between the two. There is that old canard that it is not really ice unless you can look down at it and somebody resembling you looks back.

The surface of hard-pack is minimally granular and you can still get some control by edging. However, when skiing on real ice, glare ice, or black ice, any attempt to edge your skis can be disastrous. A controlled slide on flattened skis is about the best one can do until you get to snow or a granular surface in order to be able to turn or stop. The idea that you can make a "hockey stop" on real ice is good, if you're wearing ice skates. Can it work on skis? Possibly, if you can ski in a horizontal position as some ski racers nearly do, but not for recreational skiing. Your aim is to remain upright while skiing. The other position is for sleeping.

Skiers in the Eastern United States and Canada have always bragged about their ability to handle ice. They ridicule skiers in the West who can ski their "champagne powder" but are totally inept on ice or hard-pack. *No ice?* I remember the first time I skied in Squaw Valley, California. I came down at the end of the day past a sign that read "DANGER—ICY CONDITIONS" and, after skiing over a twenty-yard patch of hard-pack, I was reminded that this was what we skied on most of the time in the East. We called it "Vermont powder!"

Yes, there is ice in Vail; not hard-pack but real *ice*—in April! When the snow melts during an April day and freezes overnight, it becomes *ice.* Most of it is excellently groomed; however, the grooming doesn't reach the approaches to the lift lines. I was skiing with the Ski Club of Great Britain (yes, in Vail) one April. Some of the chairlift lines were icy, and we were well aware of our responsibility to ski slowly to these approaches so as not to knock down the skier ahead. We were headed to Blue Sky Basin, that magnificent ten-year-old extension, through the back bowls. The approach to the Skyline Express lift was exceptionally icy and, unlike most chairlift lines, it was on a decline, not an incline. Great care was required not to slam into or run over the skier ahead.

Alas, just after I entered the line, a woman, out of control, skidded, slammed into me, and we both went down in a heap. I was stunned, and it took me a few minutes to recover as my assaulter, who was on top of me, got up. I remained lying on my side. When the club leader asked if I was okay, I thought I was, and though I was stunned momentarily, I looked up at this woman and was stunned all over again. She was stunning.

The leader asked me if he could let the woman go and, still in a semistupor, I agreed. He released her, took no name, no address, no information at all—a complete absence of responsibility? Not that I would have made any claim against her, other than requesting that she help me with dinner that night. Though I only had one functioning arm, I was not completely armless, and I certainly was harmless.

When I tried to get up by first pushing down with my left arm, I couldn't. I had a broken clavicle. I firmly believe that all things, both good and bad, come in threes. This was my third broken bone in three years after having lived seventy-seven years without even one.

I couldn't condemn the ski club leader as entirely irresponsible. After I went through a myriad of tests at the hospital, he picked me up, packed me up, and shipped me back home. That was true *responsibility*!

"I'M TOO OLD TO LEARN TO SKI!"

It was 1975 and we were now into our third year of skiing. I was with my two sons, Jamie (eleven) and Michael (ten), and we were on the chairlift coming up from Mid-Vail. Suddenly they screamed, "Daddy, look, LOOK!" as they pointed toward two guys and a gal skiing down wearing nothing but ski boots and gloves. It was the ultimate performance in spring skiing. It was the year of the *streakers!*

Yet for me, it was not the most notable happening of the day. After the boys left their ancient forty-eight-year-old father for some more challenging runs, I found myself on the chairlift with someone who seemed old enough to be *my* dad. We skied down together and I had to admire how well he skied. When we got back on the lift I said, "Do you mind if I ask how old you are?"

"I'm seventy-one."

"You ski very well. You must be skiing a long time."

"About a year." I was amazed. "Where do you live?" I asked.

"Miami Beach."

Fascinated, I asked him where he learned to ski. "In Vail last year." Then, incredulously, I inquired, "Why does a seventy-year-old man from Florida come to Colorado to learn to ski?"

"It wasn't my intention to come here to learn to ski," he replied. "My son, a doctor, was attending a medical seminar here last April. He thought it would be a good opportunity for us to spend some time together, so he invited me to join him. With nothing to do while he was in his sessions and caught up in the delight on the faces of skiers, I decided to give it a try. Even with the hassle of renting the equipment and signing up for lessons, I fell in love with this wonderful activity."

This seventy-one-year-old Floridian and his story have become my answer to anyone who says, "I'm too old to ski."

Some of us seniors have a special way of appreciating the collateral benefits of this sport, through skiing slowly and making many stops. This system, thrust upon us by natural aging, enables us to truly appreciate a cloudless blue sky, snow in its great variety, falling white flakes and crystals, the wind rustling through the trees, and fabulous mountain views. These elements all add a spiritual quality to the invigorating and exhilarating sensation of this magical glide through the snow.

It isn't easy to find a senior who doesn't have at least one physical impairment. Arthritis abounds, affecting hips, knees, backs and ankles. Replacements of hips, knees and even shoulders are quite common. There are even some skiers with "tennis elbows" who have never played tennis, but got them from the way they planted their ski poles. Many have breathing problems, so carry inhalers and deal with high altitudes by staying a day or two at an intermediate altitude, such as mile-high Denver, before skiing at Aspen Highlands, which has an altitude of over two miles

In many ways, skiing is more forgiving than other sports such as tennis, with its sudden stops and starts on not-so-forgiving surfaces. Even when skiing under control, as most experienced seniors do, unseen obstacles, like rocks or tree roots, can cause a fall. Fortunately, in most cases you fall on the pillow softness of the snow or slide on not-so-hard hard-pack (erroneously referred to as ice). Most tennis players will give up tennis years before they give up skiing.

So I say to those with or without replacement hips, knees, or whatever, "It's never, yes, *never,* too late to learn to ski, and you will—yes, you *can*—feel younger.

MISCONCEPTIONS AND
A MISSED CONNECTION

"All I needed to do to find you at the club was to look for the ambulance."

That was my tennis partner's wisecrack about the periodic episodes during a game when my back would go into spasm and the slightest movement would be excruciating. As with many jokes, it had an element of truth.

These attacks began in my early twenties and had been diagnosed as partially herniated (slipped) discs in my spine. After many consultations with neurologists and orthopedists concerning treatment, it came down to a choice of one of three possibilities: a careful sedentary life; surgery to fuse the vertebrae; or develop my musculature with physical therapy and/or take up a sport. Recommended sports were swimming, running, bicycling, even tennis. Skiing was out of the question; it was not for anyone with a bad back!

I decided on the physical therapy and tennis combination and joined Shelter Rock Tennis Club on Long Island. Initially, it was a successful day when I *walked* off the court. The remark about finding me by looking for an ambulance was an exaggeration, but, quite often, I couldn't even complete an hour of tennis.

Even though the spasms occurred regularly, and on average, I would be laid up about twice a year for two weeks at a time, I kept playing tennis. As my game improved, the number of club members I played with also increased, but everyone knew about my bad back.

Returning from Switzerland and skiing in Zermatt in April 1972, I triumphantly reported to my friends at the club that I had taken up skiing. "Skiing! It's so dangerous. How can you ski with that back of yours?" I could only reply, "I can't ski without it."

The concept of skiing being too hazardous and "out of the question" for someone with a bad back was the first of many misconceptions about skiing. Yes, certainly extreme skiing such as illustrated in Warren Miller's and other films that show skiers jumping off cliffs and skiing down couloirs can be dangerous. But not normal recreational skiing; it's certainly not as disabling as tennis can be.

I was so taken with skiing that I didn't consider any risk. Amazingly, the movements didn't seem to bother my back at all. Quite the contrary. Over the years, I discovered that recreational skiing is a much more forgiving sport than tennis, which involves a variety of movements including sudden stops, turning, twisting, and reversing direction. Injuries to the knees, hips, back and shoulders are common. Many of the same movements and appendages are also involved in skiing, but because you're dealing with a different surface, the body's reaction is different. Snow, whether powder, hard-pack or granular, produces sliding, gliding, skimming or floating action, which is so much kinder to the knees, hips and back than the action in tennis.

Tennis also has a variety of surfaces: grass, clay, Har-Tru, as well as many hard courts. One surface is less kind than the other, but none is as comfortable as any of the ski surfaces.

In the late '90s, I practically stopped playing tennis because of arthritis in my hips. When the time came that I couldn't sleep on either side, replacing the hips became a "must." On April 24, 2000, I had a bilateral hip replacement. My surgeon, Dr. Eugene Krauss, convinced me that, even though I was seventy-three years old, it was better to replace both hips at the same time and not endure rehabilitation twice. I asked him if I would have any problem in skiing. "Where do you ski?" he asked. I told him of many resorts, but he stopped me when I mentioned St. Moritz. "After three or four months you'll have no problem, especially in Switzerland. I'll ski with you in St. Moritz."

After seventeen days in the hospital, including fourteen in rehabilitation, I walked out (no wheelchair) with just two canes. Dr. Krauss was right in recommending that I have both hips done at the same time—but I'm still waiting to ski with him in St. Moritz.

By August, I was hitting balls with our tennis pro, and I started to plan a Thanksgiving ski trip to Utah. I decided to try the Canyons, not far from Salt Lake City, and thought it best to go with an instructor the first day. Jo Garuccio, one of the best in Utah, volunteered. As we got off the chairlift at the top, there was a line of snowboarders about ten yards in front of us. We had to stop. We went into a wedge (snowplow) to make a sudden stop and avoid crashing into them. Jo scolded them for putting up this blockade. I became delirious . . . deliriously happy . . . for I had just done the snowplow, one of the most elementary things in skiing. Before my surgery, I was never able to do that successfully because of my arthritic hips. Because of that, even though I had taken an instructor's course, I was never eligible to teach a beginner.

The method of teaching beginners is the ATM, the American Teaching Method, which starts with the wedge. Not only could I now accomplish that, but every other skiing technique was easier. Jo showed me that with the new parabolic-shaped skis all I had to do before making the turn was to relax my downhill leg. This was the only technique she showed me, but I will always remember her for instructing me in the art of relaxation while skiing.

With all the concern about my hips, I had completely forgotten about my back. The two-week, twice-a-year episodes of spasms had vanished. I never made the connection between this nonoccurrence and skiing until very recently, when I started to write this book. It has been at least twenty-five years since the last spasmodic episode. My midsection, my stomach, buttocks, and quadriceps muscles have become so strong that they have, undoubtedly, prevented the discs from slipping.

I may have missed that connection between skiing and my back problem, but I don't miss the spasms. What skiing has done for my well-being has been amazingly remarkable.

GETTING YOUNGER AS WE AGE

When I'm asked my age I sometimes reply, "Averaging in the age of my new parts—my replacement hips are only eleven years old, one knee is still an infant, my coronary stents are seven, my dentures three and my hearing aids are two—then I'm about thirty-nine." I probably have more legitimacy to that facetious claim than Jack Benny.

Alas, I think that ski areas have taken this joke too seriously. During the last ten years they have consistently raised lift ticket prices for seniors over the age of seventy. Once upon a time, Vail gave free lift tickets to skiers of that age. But by 2008, the best a seventy-plus senior could do was to buy a ten-day pass for $479, averaging about $48 per day. Single-day passes are, of course, much higher.

For years, most ski resorts in France allowed those over seventy to ski free. The justification for giving free or discounted passes to those who are seventy-plus is the belief that they ski fewer hours and use the lifts fewer times. I turned seventy in April 1997, and when I went to the ticket window in Courchevel in 1998 to get my free lift pass, I was told that the age had been raised to seventy-five.

Among American ski areas that no longer give free passes to us seniors, in addition to Vail, are Hunter Mountain, New York; Park City, Utah; and Telluride, Colorado. However, if you're eighty-plus, you can still ski free in Taos, New Mexico, and if over seventy-five, you can ski free in most areas in France.

"We're not getting older, we're getting better" can be amended to "we're not getting older, we're getting younger; there are more of us skiing, and we're getting better at it!"

SKI CLUBS

Ski clubs are a wonderful boon to a wonderful sport. Practically all of them arrange group trips and handle the booking of hotels at special group rates, getting both rental equipment and lift passes at a discount. On many flights, both domestic and international, the clubs arrange for special rates as well as transfers from the airport to the resort.

Club membership can match you with skiers at all levels of ability, and making friends for a lifetime happens time and again.

Over the years, I have joined several clubs: The Ski Club of Great Britain, the 70+ Ski Club, the Miami Ski Club, the Over the Hill Gang, and the Best of Times (formerly the Eastern 50+) Ski Club. Starting with the oldest of these exceptional clubs, following is a skiing history from the turn of one century to the turn of the next.

SKI CLUB OF GREAT BRITAIN

SCGB was founded on May 6, 1903, at the Café Royal by seven "ski runners" who vowed to "foster a healthful and delightful addition to the recognized sports of the country."

Among its many achievements, in 1911 the club organized the first International Downhill Race in Austria and, in 1921, the first National Championships in Switzerland. The club also established the rules for racing for the International Ski Federation in 1930.

Currently, the club boasts approximately thirty-four thousand members. Past and present members include a host of celebrities and royalty, not only of Great Britain but from many other countries. In addition to British royalty such as the Prince of Wales, Duke of Kent, the Duchess of York, and Prince Edward, membership has included princes of the Netherlands and Romania; kings of Norway and Belgium; the Aga Khan, and the Shah of Persia. Celebrity members include Arthur Conan Doyle and the famed skier Graham Bell. Lord Dowling, the Earl of Limerick, and Alan Blackshaw are past presidents.

As with most other ski clubs, the Ski Club of Great Britain arranges affordable group trips (principally to the Alps) and discounts for rental equipment, lift tickets, and other services. Its Web site, www.skiclub.co.uk, receives more than 350,000 hits per month

What makes SCGB so special among ski clubs is its repping service, established back in 1928. Representatives of the club, referred to as Ski Club Leaders, are stationed at thirty-seven resorts in Europe and North America. They undergo intensive training in order to achieve a high standard in mountain craft, first aid, safety, and leadership skills. They form groups of skiers of comparable abilities, select the best runs, and not only lead skiers on groomed and off-piste runs, but also familiarize their members with the specific offerings of the resorts at which they're based.

Though their skiing skills are of the highest order, the leaders don't compete with instructors at the resorts. They do not instruct. Their on-slope duties are principally of group leadership. They are chosen for their sociability to ensure that the member's precious time on the snow is enhanced by the daily après-ski get-together at a hotel, restaurant, or wherever.

Membership is from all corners of the UK. And yes, there is now the huge total of forty-one American members. The thirty-seven resorts where the ski leaders are stationed are in Switzerland (nine), France (eleven), Austria (five), Canada (four), Italy (two), Andorra in Spain (one), and USA (five). I have skied with them in France (Courchevel, Meribel, Tignes, Val d'Isère); Italy (Cervinia); Switzerland (Davos, Grindelwald, Klosters, Wengen, St. Moritz, Zermatt); and in the USA (Aspen/Snowmass, Vail/Beaver Creek, Breckenridge).

The uniqueness and magnitude of the club ski leader program is unmatched by any other ski club worldwide. I have the utmost appreciation for this service, and as an American, though I have been to resorts where I didn't use the service, it has been most comforting to know that it was there and even more comforting to know that the leader spoke a language somewhat like my own.

ADDENDUM

In 1997, the year that Caroline Stuart Taylor became CEO of SCGB, we both had the idea of making Americans more aware of the club and the club leadership service. I helped arrange for an American tour operator to offer membership in SCGB with their ski packages, thereby providing a leader of an English-speaking group with whom to ski and socialize, for just the club's nominal dues.

The performance of the tour operator was disappointing, enlisting very few members. I still think the idea is valid, and with a better tour operator and good promotion, American membership could be substantial.

70+ SKI CLUB

If you are over seventy years of age, where is the best place to ski? If you're a member of the 70+ Ski Club, the answer to that question is *everywhere!*

Since its inception in 1977, this ski club has had many trips to the Alps in Europe, the Andes in South America, the Southern Alps of New Zealand, and most of the major resorts in the USA and Canada. I was fortunate to be able to ski with the club in Bariloche and Las Leñas in Argentina; and Coronet Peak, the Remarkables and Mt. Hutt in New Zealand. At Valle Nevado in Chile, the U.S. ambassador to that country flew into the resort by helicopter to meet with members of the club. Valle Nevado is connected to two other ski resorts in Chile—El Colorado and La Parva—making this a favorite South American resort because of its proximity to the major city of Santiago.

No resort is too distant for the 70+ Ski Club, and no skier is too old to be a member. Since 1977, the club has registered over twenty-one thousand members; currently, the roster lists more than 1,500 over 80, and 125 over 90. The second active member in the club's history to reach the age of one hundred did so in July 2010.

Three generations of the Lambert family have managed the club. Lloyd Lambert, born in 1901 in Binghamton, New York, was a pioneer in the sport of skiing. His passion began in 1915 when he was fourteen, on a pair of pine boards purchased at a hardware store for $1.98. At the age of ninety-five, he was still skiing and still carrying his ancient bamboo ski poles.

Lambert's activities began as a National Ski Patroller. Later he became a ski columnist and the first radio broadcaster focusing only on that sport. He was instrumental in the founding of many ski associations and clubs. In this area, his founding of the 70+ Ski Club in 1977 was a statement to the skiing world that those skiers who had reached the biblical age of three score and ten were a factor to be reckoned with.

Skiing came into prominence in the United States in the 1930s. In 1938, there were only 113 ski lifts in the entire country; most were draglifts, known in the Alps as Schleplifts. No more than ten were overhead cable lifts, three of which were chairlifts constructed in Sun Valley, Idaho, the first of their kind. By 1955, there were more than two hundred overhead cable lifts. The sport of skiing in the U.S. was not just *lifted*, it was *sky rocketing*!

Much of the impetus came from the ski troops of the Tenth Mountain Division of World War II. Among those most prominent was Peter Seibert, who founded the resort which has become one of the most popular in the U.S.—Vail, Colorado.

The 1950s proved to be the turning point for skiing in the U.S. The occasional dabbling of just a few in this relatively new activity has since become the recreational winter sport of thousands. Lloyd Lambert's weekly fifteen-minute radio program was eagerly listened to in the Eastern United States. Ultimately, his founding of the Ski Museum at Hunter Mountain in Upstate New York became a vital element in his most visionary creation.

In 1976, at the age of seventy-five, Lloyd became dismayed that so many of his friends were hanging up their skis. He discovered that they weren't dropping out because of age or fitness but because of their pocketbooks. The cost of lift tickets had steadily increased and would soon make them unaffordable. He then had the idea that turned out to be the most important contribution to the world of senior skiing: *discounts for seniors!*

He formed the 70+ Ski Club, the only one restricted to skiers seventy and over, with its primary aim to obtain discounts for its members. In 1977, he persuaded Orville and Izzy Slutzky, the co-owners of the facility at Hunter, to offer free skiing to members of the club, the youngest of whom, of course, were septuagenarians. Naturally, these members didn't come alone. They brought their children and grandchildren, all of whom paid full price. As a result, through these full prices combined with food, drink, equipment rentals, etc., Hunter Mountain's revenues grew at an exceptional rate.

A charitable decision turned out to be a major marketing miracle, and that first year, thirty more ski areas in the East joined in and offered free or steeply discounted tickets to seniors. Today, more than two hundred ski resorts worldwide employ this marketing strategy. Annually, the 70+ Ski Club offers a list of areas that give free or discounted tickets to seniors.

Lloyd Lambert's efforts in achieving free or discounted lift tickets, together with organizing trips all over the world, brought the membership to over eight thousand. The numbers were often overwhelming, and Lambert said more than once, "If I had thought it would be this big, I never would have started it."

Although he allowed his expenses on major trips to be paid, he never profited monetarily from the club. It was basically a voluntary contribution to the world of senior skiing. His "profit" was the satisfaction he received in his rare achievements for the sport of skiing.

His honors were numerous, including special awards at Klosters in Switzerland and Cortina in Italy, and the North American Ski Journalists' Award, the *Golden Quill*. He was featured on sixty TV shows worldwide as the leading exponent of senior skiing.

Lloyd passed away in 1998 at the age of ninety-seven. His son Richard became the Executive Director but wasn't able to join the club since he was underage. Dick had a different idea as to why people quit skiing: it isn't because of fitness, age, or affordability, but a matter of camaraderie. People stopped skiing when they had no one to ski with. His emphasis on that aspect brought a special sociability that now permeates the club quite happily.

When Dick passed away his son, Richard Jr., assumed the directorship. He is also underage and has a few years before he can join, which he is looking forward to doing when the timing is right.

At the turn of the last century, life expectancy in the United States was 49.2 years. At the turn of this new century, it was 77.5 years, a remarkable sixty-three percent increase. Statistics also show that the number of centenarians grows seven percent per year.

In this twenty-first century, if we are able to overcome planet-threatening disasters such as a nuclear holocaust, pandemic disease, world hunger, water deprivation and global warming, it is possible that life expectancy could climb at a similar rate to that in the twentieth century. If so, by the end of this century one could anticipate living to the ripe old age of 130.

Is it also possible that efforts to counter global warming could actually produce a condition of global cooling, giving us snowfalls similar to those we had at the turn of the twentieth century? Would it not then be feasible that some future generation of the Lambert family would form another club for older skiers—the 100+ Ski Club? (Don't discount it!)

OTHGI (OVER THE HILL
GANG INTERNATIONAL)

In days of yore, reaching the age of fifty meant the beginning of what was then known as "the golden years" and was heralded as the best of times. This followed the earlier words of consolation for growing older, "Life begins at forty." But then it was realized that becoming fifty meant that you were "over the hill."

I never could figure out what "hill" people were talking about. It seemed to me that if you were able to climb a hill it meant that you've accomplished something in life. Recognition that those of us who were able to continue skiing after reaching the age of fifty had indeed achieved something major was the motivation behind the establishment of a special ski club, named the Over the Hill Gang (OTHG) when it was formed in 1977.

Over the years membership grew until it became one of the largest ski clubs in the United States, with more than six thousand members. Ultimately, its appeal eventually extended to Canada and overseas, mandating a name change to Over the Hill Gang International (OTHGI). "International" also aptly describes the worldwide destinations of club-sponsored ski trips to such places as the Alps in Italy and Switzerland; the Andes in South America; and even New Zealand. It doesn't limit its activities to skiing; there have been biking trips in Andalusia, Thailand, and England; golf in Slovenia and Guatemala; and adventure in Machu Picchu in Peru.

Unique among most ski clubs based in the United States, OTHGI formed regional chapters that arranged their own trips, mainly to domestic destinations such as Aspen and Vail in Colorado; Snowbird, Alta, and Park City in Utah; and Heavenly Valley and Squaw Valley in Nevada and California. My introduction to OTHGI was through the Eastern Chapter which had annual trips to Vail in December, Sun Valley in January, and Aspen in March.

From its inception, camaraderie has been the most significant element in all OTHGI's activities. It has often been said that friends made through skiing become friends for life, and, though this may well be true of all ski clubs, OTHGI emphasizes it in all its publicity—unsurpassed camaraderie among its six-thousand-plus members.

Another major feature of the club is its ability to obtain major discounts for lift passes, lodging, and equipment rentals, mainly in Colorado where the club is based. Most importantly are its free guided ski days in many Colorado resorts such as Aspen, Vail, Breckenridge, Keystone, and Snowmass. These are usually one day per week when skiers of equal ability are formed into groups to learn about the mountain.

THE BEST OF TIMES, et al

In September 2005, the managers of OTHGI, Dennis and Sherrie Beasley, and Arthur and Denise Foley, sent a letter to all chapter members expressing their heartfelt regret that the chapters had to be dissolved. The dissolution was necessary because of an inability to obtain adequate insurance coverage for the chapters. However, since more than seventy percent of its members were not members of individual chapters, OTHGI would carry on.

As a result, most of the chapters formed independent ski clubs. The Eastern Chapter became the Eastern 50+ Ski Club; in 2010, the club was renamed the Best of Times Ski Club (BOTSC). It is closely aligned with the Capital Golden Ski Club based in Washington DC and the Connecticut-based Top Notch Ski Club. The plethora of opportunities offered by this alliance is immense, covering ski trips to all parts of the U.S. as well as many trips abroad. Spawned by the Over the Hill Gang International, these clubs are *golden, top notch*, and always give all its members *the best of times*.

MIAMI SKI CLUB

The perfect definition of an anomaly—a peculiarity, a rarity, an oddity—is the Miami Ski Club.

It has always been a source of amazement to me that a ski club from the Deep South became the largest ski club in the United States. (See the episode "We Killed Him" as to how I joined the club and, because of that, how it almost cost me my life.)

The Miami Ski Club was founded in 1968 and is one of the oldest and, improbably, still one of the largest ski clubs in the country. In the mid-1980s the Florida Ski Council was formed, comprising seventeen local clubs. Council membership includes clubs from both coasts, the interior and the panhandle. The individual trips of each club are publicized to all the members of the council, and all are invited to participate.

The Miami Ski Club bills itself as "A Club for All Seasons"—and more. In addition to offering ski events, it is a dynamic social organization with happy hours weekly, cultural events, and nonskiing outings including bicycle rides, kayak trips, concerts, and travel to destinations both in the U.S. and abroad. These trips have spanned the four corners of the world including such far-flung places as Russia, Australia, New Zealand, China, Vietnam, Egypt, Jordan, and most of Europe. Though they have not yet reached the moon, I understand that it is under consideration.

Primarily, club membership is from South Florida, but there have also been members throughout the United States with at least two from New York. Inexplicably, there are also members from abroad. It is not only a club for all seasons; it is also a club for all who would join.

Does it snow in Florida? Of course! In the eighteenth century, there were two recorded snowfalls. The one in 1774 was called "extraordinary white rain." On January 11, 1800, there was a snowfall of over five inches just north of Jacksonville and was one of fifteen recorded snowfalls in the entire nineteenth century, including mid-February during the Great Blizzard of 1899 when a *huge* amount of snow—four inches!—fell at Lake Butler.

Reports have it that there were twenty snowfall events in Florida in the twentieth century and, so far, early in the twenty-first, there have already been at least nine.

Is there skiing in Florida? Absolutely! You can water ski in every part of the state, on both coasts, the panhandle, and even parts of the interior.

Is there a difference between snow skiing and water skiing? Without a doubt! If you have ever skied on snow, there can be only one thing to say: *vive la différence!*

MOST EXHILARATING

I said, "Skiing is the second most exhilarating thing I've done in my lifetime." She said, "Well, what was the first?"

Ouch! In all the years I've made that statement no one ever asked! I was perplexed and tongue-tied, not quite knowing how to respond to this new acquaintance. I mumbled, "Umm—selling lamps. I used to be a lamp manufacturer." She seemed puzzled and said only, "Oh." That was the end of the conversation as we got off the chairlift, and I thought the whole thing had gone over her head.

My wife and I had met this couple only the day before. We were skiing in Solitude, Utah, where the Honeycomb Canyon presents one of the greatest powder runs in the Rockies—truly exhilarating! We made a date with Inez and her husband Marvin to ski the next day at Snowbird.

I was awakened early the next morning by the ringing of the phone and answered in a drowsy stupor, coming out of a deep sleep. It was Inez. "Oh," she said, "did I disturb you? Were you selling lamps?" So much for "over the head!"

She called to say they wanted to ski at Alta, which we did that day and Snowbird the next two days. It was a lovely Thanksgiving holiday.

Our family then went to Val d'Isère in France for Christmas, where we enjoyed another memorable skiing holiday. After Joan went home with the boys, I went to Zermatt where I had promised to meet some friends from my tennis club.

During lunch one day, I made the remark that skiing was the second most exhilarating thing I've done and recounted my exchange with Inez. No one at the table had to ask what was the first, but an Englishman at the next table leaned over. "Excuse me," he said, "but I couldn't help overhearing what you were saying. Isn't it a shame what AIDS has done to the lamp industry?"

Then and there, I decided to join the Ski Club of Great Britain—not necessarily for skiing, but for great English humor!

One of my early goals when I started skiing was to ski in South America during our North American summer. The 70+ Ski Club advertised a trip to Bariloche in Argentina. When I called to inquire about the trip, I was asked my age. Since I was only sixty-six, I was told that I wasn't old enough. "I don't want to join the club," I said, "I just want to go on the trip." A few days later a club rep called and said they had had a meeting and decided that I could go as a guest.

In the evening of the first day, about eight of us were sitting around a table telling of our skiing experiences. When it was my turn I said that I only started skiing when I turned forty-five but that "it's the second most exhilarating . . ." One of the older members came over and put his arm around my shoulder. "Listen, Sonny-boy," he said, "as you grow older it will inevitably become the first." So far, I guess I'm not old enough.

THE FLIPPER

In this story, a "flipper" is not a dolphin, a TV show, or a politician who constantly changes his political positions. This flipper is a temporary removable partial denture, so named because it can be easily removed with just a flip of a finger.

Having lost four of my lower teeth and awaiting the installation of a permanent bridge, I was wearing such a device on one of my trips to St. Moritz.

On the way down from Corviglia to St. Moritz one day, I was skiing past a beginner's class when one woman lost her edge and fell right into my path. I somersaulted over her and had a world-class wipeout. Both of my skis released, and I was lying in the snow in a big heap, in a prenatal position.

Fortunately, neither one of us was hurt. In a great deal of distress, the woman came over to where I was lying and apologized profusely. What seemed like a dozen times, she moaned, "I'm sorry, I'm so sorry. Are you hurt?"

I removed my gloves and proceeded to examine my arms and legs. I turned my head away from her, and with the index finger of my left hand, I flipped out my flipper into my right hand. Then I turned toward her and said, "I think I'm all right, but do I have all my teeth?"

I guess cruelty has no bounds—even in the snow!

PET PEEVES

There is no doubt in my mind that when it comes to skiing, I have been extremely spoiled.

After that first day in Zermatt, the family returned home, but I had to drive down to the Italian city of Florence on business. On the way, I took advantage of the opportunity to stop in Verbier for a few days, where I took some excellent ski lessons. I continued to be enraptured.

The family returned to Zermatt for the Christmas holiday, and subsequently, we added France and Austria to our destinations twice a year, including Easter. Between these trips, we did a great deal of skiing in the North American East. It soon became evident that there were notable differences between the Alps and the North American East, especially in the ambience. In addition, as I became more proficient and self-confident, I soon developed what I now term *pet peeves.*

SERVICE OR SELF-SERVICE?

Waiter! Waiter! Where is the waiter?

If you stop for lunch at an American ski resort and expect to be served, you might have to wait a long time since almost all eating establishments on American ski slopes are self-service cafeterias. Even among those that do have service, very few serve outdoors, and it would be exceptional to have more than one such in any resort.

The scarcity of midmountain restaurants with service in American ski resorts is astonishing and one of my major pet peeves. To sit at a table on the terrace or deck of a midmountain restaurant and have lunch served to you is one of the delights of skiing. Stretching your legs after skiing all morning on a sunny day, enjoying the always spectacular mountain views while you experience good service, you have a little bit of heaven in the snow.

One of these little bits of heaven in the U.S. is in Aspen Highlands, Colorado, aptly named Cloud Nine Bistro. Another is the historic Roundhouse in Sun Valley, Idaho, a favorite of so many celebrities since its introduction in the late 1930s. Alta and Solitude in Utah boast midmountain full-service restaurants. There are others but they are few and far between. Most full service restaurants in the U.S. can be found at the base of the mountains.

By contrast, let's look at a few resorts in the Alps. Zermatt has thirty-eight midmountain restaurants, all accessible by ski. (There are a few self-service cafeterias, but they're as rare in the Alps as full-service restaurants are in the U.S.) Most offer service both indoors and out, on stone terraces or wood decks.

Among my favorites are the Sunnega Restaurant with its large semicircular terrace; the Kulm Hotel Restaurant at the top of Gornergrat with its sun-drenched terrace facing Monte Rosa; Grunsee, with a balcony terrace on the White Hare Run from Hohtälli to Gant; Fluhalp, on the run to Gant from the top of Rothorn, which boasts live music. And there's Chez Vrony in Findeln, rated one of the best in the Alps. Each has its own special character, but they all share one thing in common: fantastic views of a fantastic mountain, the Matterhorn! And one other great treat: the brilliant sun!

Sunnega Restaurant, one of the author's favorites, accessible to nonskiers at the top of the funicular

On the other side of the Matterhorn is the Italian town of Cervinia, which can be skied to from Zermatt and where one can enjoy a similar array of midmountain restaurants. My favorite is Chalet Etoile, just above Plan Maison, the center of the resort. It is managed by a free-spirited Swedish woman, Ulla di Frassy, who has a team of dazzling waitresses dressed in costumes, all wearing lovely hats and featuring a group known as the Four Blondes. Oh yes, the food is also good.

In France, Les Trois Vallées, comprised of eight interconnected ski resorts, probably has more full-service midmountain restaurants than all American ski resorts combined. My favorite on the Bellecôte piste is the Courcheneige, with a wood deck a little larger than a basketball court. Its great mountain views can be gazed at directly or through reflections in the windows of the hotel. It has a marvelous buffet, plus table service and live music.

Michelin-rated restaurants are world leaders in culinary delights. In all of New York City, there are only five. Astonishingly, there are five nestled in the heart of Les Trois Vallées, all accessible by ski. I have been to just one, La Bouitte (The Little House) in Saint Martin de Belleville. It seemed quite odd to be served by a waiter in formal attire while sitting outdoors in an alcove surrounded by snow. It was truly *haute cuisine!*

Although the French have produced some great skiers, it can be argued that the national pastime is not skiing, but dining, even on the slopes.

Probably the average amount of time American skiers take for lunch is twenty minutes. Europeans take at least an hour and, sometimes, as many as two. For many of them, that's what skiing is all about. If there were more midmountain restaurants with service in America, perhaps we, too, could begin to appreciate dining on the slopes!

There is a snow field at the top of Mount Mannlichen in Switzerland called the Beach, complete with beach chairs. After some hearty skiing in the morning, one can stretch out on a chair with ski boots on and relax in the sun. In such a moment I also say, "That's what skiing is all about!"

A POLL ON SKI POLES

There are two issues about ski poles that need to be addressed: how to use them, and how to hold them.

Back in the 1970s, ski schools were using a new technique to teach beginners how to parallel turn. With the Graduated Length Method (GLM), beginners learned to make parallel turns *before* any of those old-fashioned things like snow-plows (wedge turns), stemming (stem Christies), sideslipping, etc.

Before the advent of the new shaped skis, parallel turns were made by "unweighting." This is a technique of first bending and then, as you came up from the bend at the beginning of the turn, the weight would come off the skis and make them easy to turn in unison—a parallel turn. Beginners would start on very short skis, much lighter in weight than traditional skis; the weight would come off the skis very easily and, as a consequence, achieving the paradise of parallel skiing was easy. Gradually, during the first week of the GLM method, the length of the skis would be increased and soon, beginners were parallel skiing on the "bunny slopes." They had conquered the world! They had accomplished this without using their ski poles and were probably wondering what the darn things were for anyway.

"Pole planting," an essential for intermediate, advanced, and expert skiing, was usually introduced in the second week of GLM instruction. However, since most students had already conquered that world of parallel skiing and were venturing onto intermediate slopes, few bothered to learn how and when to plant their poles, to say nothing of other elements that make a complete skier.

Riding up on a chairlift, I was always amused—as well as bothered—to see these GLM skiers with poles in their hands without a clue as to how to use them. They always reminded me of those who get a good book, read a review, and never read the book.

Though my intent was not to write a book of instruction, clearly, I can't resist. Proper pole planting requires strong wrist action to help guard against the tendency of pulling the hand back after planting the pole. If your poling resembles rowing a boat, then boating should be your sport, not skiing. Not only is "rowing a boat" one of my pet peeves, it can also be dangerous. By pulling your hand back past your hip after planting the pole, you can completely lose control. It's OK when you're on the flat or a cat-track, but not when skiing downhill.

Holding the ski poles is another issue. Except for some made with extreme pistol grips, ski poles have straps. These were designed for your hand to go through this loop before you grasp the handle of the pole. To do this properly, your thumb goes *over* both thongs of the strap; otherwise, a fall could produce a badly sprained thumb. Have you got that? *Well, forget it!* It is safer, on all counts, *not* to put your hands through the straps.

Over the years, I have found that the benefits of *not* putting one's hands through the straps far outweigh the advantages of doing so. There is obvious danger when skiing in the trees with pole straps on your wrists. Less obvious, but still a danger, is the possibility of the basket of the pole snagging on any number of objects such as clothing, another's skis, lift apparatus, etc. Any of these can result in serious injury to wrists, elbows, shoulders, or the entire arm.

In a fall, ski poles don't "run away" as skis did in the past before the advent of ski brakes. However, when hands are put through the straps, there is a "windmilling" injury potential similar to that of skis of yesteryear, which had ankle straps instead of modern-day brakes. Now that new technology has released us from the danger of injury by the windmilling, why do we continue to be shackled to ski poles by having straps around our wrists?

The minimal support to the wrists provided by straps won't match the wrist strength achieved after a few days of holding the pole straps against the handle in the palm of the hand. Also, while poling on the flat, the leverage in pushing forward by placing your palm on the top of the pole is much greater than that provided by the strap, which actually hinders the use of the palm.

An additional benefit is that you don't have to bother taking your hands out of the pole straps when boarding a chairlift.

Why don't I remove the straps? I need them to hang the poles up when I'm not skiing!

These past few years, I have conducted a totally unscientific poll, the result of which is that I find more and more skiers are not putting their hands through that loop. They've discovered that it can be a *loophole*!

VANQUISHED BUT NOT
ENTIRELY VANISHED

It's 5:00 p.m., rush hour in New York City. We're standing on the subway platform at 42nd Street when the train arrives and all hell breaks loose. The crowd shoves and elbows its way through the doorways onto the train. Those stories about some guys beating old ladies to a seat aren't exactly true; sometimes the old lady gets there first.

Now let's go to Zermatt in Switzerland, in 1973. We're at Riffelberg and just above the restaurant is a T-Bar lift that services a run back to Riffelberg or on to Riffelalp. The scene is not unlike the subway scene described above except that the pushing and shoving is done by people on skis employing their ski poles in their effort to get on the lift. There are no orderly lines, two abreast, for an orderly mounting of the lift. German skiers cross skis with the English, the French with the Dutch, Americans with Belgians, and on and on. It's a free-for-all. This pet peeve doesn't apply only to T-Bars, but these lifts bear the added annoyance of balancing position with the person you're paired with, especially when she is five feet tall and you are six foot two.

In 1973, skiing down from Riffelalp ended with a schuss down to the Furi cable car station, the cable car to Trockener Steg, followed by the awesome cable car to Klein Matterhorn. But wait a moment! There was no Klein Matterhorn cable car in 1973; construction didn't even start until 1976 and wasn't completed until December 1979!

So without it, how did we get to the Plateau Rosa and on to the Italian slopes in Cervinia? Easily! We took three "Schleplifts," two T-Bars and one Poma lift. Then a schuss and we were in Italy. And yes, with more and more T-Bars.

What a surprise!! The reputed playful, mischievous, independent, roguish Italians were lined up in astonishingly orderly fashion at their T-Bars. They were the souls of patience waiting their turn. Was this really Italy?

It is now 2011 and most of the T-Bars in the Alps have been replaced by chairlifts for four or six, and cable cars or gondolas that carry as many as twelve. Crowded lift lines are mainly a thing of the past as is, for some, having to deal with unbalanced T-Bars and similarly unbalanced skiers. For me, it has now become a vanishing petty pet peeve.

SNOWBOARDERS

They were speaking Portuguese. There I was, stunned, in agony on my back in the snow, and they were speaking Portuguese.

And we weren't even in Portugal. They don't have much snowboarding in Portugal.

Skiing down to the Town Lift in Park City, Utah, on a narrow track, a snowboarder pulled ahead of me and, in some strange and crazy maneuver, made a U-turn and met me head on. Or I should say "hands on," for my poles were held in front of me. The collision was a wrist bender.

The ski patrol arrived in force—there were three of them. The snowboarder was not injured but his board was rendered completely useless. I was dazed by the impact, but also outraged to have, once again (see below), been flattened by an out-of-control snowboarder within just a few days.

He was a young man, probably still in his twenties, and very apologetic. However, I was irate and told the ski patrol that I wanted to know everything about him, where he was staying, even his home address. And I wanted him to walk down to the village of Park City through the deep snow—it was only about a mile. I was going to make him pay for his carelessness.

Still very apologetic, the poor fellow said, "I'm a new snowboarder. I'm from Brazil." Just then, my dear Brazilian friend, Miguel, caught up with us and, of course, started speaking Portuguese. After I mouthed to Miguel that I was OK, he said, "Stanley, let him go, he's from my hometown." (Miguel's home town is Sao Paulo, with a population of about twenty million.) We let him go. Once I got back up and into my skis, we skied down to the village. My solace was that the snowboarder was walking.

This was the second time in a week that I was knocked down by a snowboarder; the first was in Santa Fe, New Mexico. Two wipe-outs caused by snowboarders in two different states all in one week. Surely, that must be a record.

In that same week, I skied a couple of days at Taos, New Mexico, during a notable and, for me, coincidental time. It was the first week in the history of this famous ski area that snowboarders were allowed on this fantastic terrain. It was March 19, 2008. I cancelled the free lift ticket given to seniors over eighty.

Skiing one day in Snowbird, Utah, a snowboarder came from above and crashed into me. When we both got up, he started to shout at me that I had made a bad turn which forced him to collide with me. He didn't seem to know the "rules of the road" as applied to ski slopes. Whether skier or snowboarder, the one above or behind is the responsible one, and that person is the one at fault in the event of a collision.

Yet the most spectacular snowboard accident I ever experienced was quite different. It was in Kitzbühel, Austria, where there was a very narrow and very crowded cat-track leading to one of the lifts. A young woman lost control of her snowboard and fell across the cat-track, stretched out full length, blocking everyone. There was no way to ski around her and no way to make a sudden stop. We were like bowling pins as we fell one on top of the other in a great heap—many more than ten pins. Fortunately, no one was injured. Yes, the responsible party was neither above nor behind the other skiers, but was ahead of us all. So much for rules of the road!

Snowboarding was developed in the United States in the late 1960s and 1970s. It has elements of three sports: surfing, skateboarding, and skiing. Historical records indicate that the original snowboard was called a "snurfer."

There has always been animosity between skiers and snowboarders, but less so as time goes by. Initially, ski areas were reluctant to allow snowboarders on their slopes; in 1985, only seven percent permitted them. Now over ninety-seven percent allow them and most of these areas have special terrain such as half pipes and snowboard jumps. The growth in the ratio of snowboarders to skiers has been dramatic, and the percentage of revenue received has been paramount in keeping many ski areas open. Though skiers are greatly annoyed by out-of-control snowboarders, those who understand the economics of the sport realize that ski areas need them for their very existence.

THE WARM-UP

It was called, "The Greatest Sports Moment of the Twentieth Century." The year was 1980, during the Winter Olympics at Lake Placid, New York, when the U.S. ice hockey team defeated the hugely favored USSR team and won the Gold. Five seconds before the end of the game the broadcaster, Al Michaels, shouted, "DO YOU BELIEVE IN MIRACLES?," and the game has since been known as the Miracle on Ice.

In preparation for those Olympic games, the U.S. and Swedish ski teams were training at Killington, Vermont, which had just opened the new area of Bear Mountain. It had only two runs, both black, Outer Limits and Wildfire. Outer Limits was aptly named, as it had giant moguls from top to bottom and was quite steep. Wildfire was perfect for giant slalom training.

I was skiing with Peter Jungkunst, a Swiss friend, and celebrating his birthday which was about ten days before the start of the Olympics. We went over to Bear Mountain but were only allowed to ski Outer Limits since the Olympic teams were training on Wildfire. After two runs on the gigantic bumps, our legs had turned to jelly. We decided to return early the next morning to ski the friendlier run of Wildfire before the teams arrived for training. That morning we were the first ones on the chairlift, but a few chairs behind us was Ingemar Stenmark of the Swedish team. Renowned as "The King of Slalom," he is the most successful Alpine ski racer in history. He has won eighty-six World Cup races and two Olympic gold medals.

When we got off the lift at the top, a guard standing at a rope, closing off the entry to Wildfire, told us that we couldn't ski there because Wildfire was being used for the races. I said, "I know, we're waiting for Stenmark," and as Stenmark approached, the guard lowered the rope, and Peter and I joined the skier for a warm-up run. We knew we were skiing with Stenmark, but he had no idea he was skiing with us.

To our amazement, we couldn't stay *behind* him. We couldn't ski as *slowly* as he did. He took about five or six turns, stopped for a few seconds, then maybe nine or ten turns, stopped, more turns and stops, gradually increasing the number of turns. We kept getting ahead of him until we were about halfway down, when he took off and was out of sight in seconds.

At the end of the day, I commented to Peter that I was not as tired as I usually was after skiing all day. He suggested that it might have been due to the slow warm-up. He was right! Later that month, in an article in one of the ski magazines, Stenmark wrote that he does this slow warm-up run in order to maintain his technique. Whenever I do this slow warm-up, my stamina is better and, just like Stenmark, it helps me maintain my technique.

What does all this have to do with pet peeves?

Years ago, once I had gained some proficiency in skiing, I would charge off the chairlift as fast as I could to prove how great I was. It was *macho!* It was *wrong*. Now, since the episode with Stenmark, I do this slow warm-up whenever I can. However, if I am skiing with a group and someone else is leading, he or she is often prone to ski as fast as possible, taking a long run on the first run of the day. I have to forget about the slow warm-up if I want to keep up with the group. As a result, my stamina suffers.

A very wise instructor once said, "Anyone can look good skiing fast, but you will know a really excellent skier if he or she looks good going slowly."

One of the keys to skiing fast is to perfect the technique of skiing slowly. It's a matter of control. The better you exercise control going slowly, the faster you'll be able to ski at high speeds.

Very often I will challenge a *macho* skier to a race by pointing to a spot downhill and say, "Let's have a race to that spot. *The last one wins!*"

Interestingly, my son Michael relates some advice he was given by Jean Vuarnet (son of the creator of the sunglass brand), when we were skiing in Morzine. "Jean noticed I was getting tired while skiing," Michael told me. "He mentioned that I was skiing well but making too much effort. He said, in French, 'Make the effort *not* to make an effort.' Since then I've always heeded his advice; it makes me more relaxed, and I don't get so tired anymore."

I haven't had the opportunity to discuss this with Ingemar Stenmark but I'm sure he would agree.

OLYMPIANS, INSTRUCTORS, AUTHORS, AND OTHER NOTABLES

During the thirty-nine years I have been skiing, I've had the pleasure of meeting some extraordinary individuals, many of whom are mentioned throughout this book.

There are episodes involving personages such as the great scientist Albert Einstein, the distinguished journalist Burnett Hershey, and Dick Bass, who at the time of his achievement was the oldest person to reach the summit of Mt. Everest.

Olympians such as Jean-Claude Killy, Alberto Tomba, and Ingemar Stenmark have received more than honorable mention in these pages, as have the renowned filmmaker Warren Miller and a major instructor who has taught skiing on several continents, Heidi Knaus.

There are a few more skiers with whom I have had unique relationships. The following pages tell those stories.

CAROL GRANT SULLIVAN

"It was insanely steep. There was no room for error."

Brian, Carol and their guide, Kees, alighted from the chairlift at twelve thousand feet and began their climb. They were headed for the summit of Cerro Torrecallas, a mountain just short of fourteen thousand feet above the ski resort Las Leñas in the Argentine Andes.

Carol had anticipated a climb of about an hour, but the snow was so deep it took over three hours to reach the summit. Resting at the top, the three of them gazed upon a vista of snow-capped peaks in all directions; it almost seemed as if they were on another planet.

In the extreme backcountry skiing world of Brian and Carol Sullivan, this was a peak of a magnitude they had never before confronted. They faced a descent more extreme than any they had ever skied. It required a drop of more than forty-five degrees off a cornice, a crusty ridge, into a steep couloir and then a narrow chute bordered by rocky crags on each side. The line would then go into a slightly wider couloir, a nearly vertical corridor, before reaching a bowl of deep powder where they could "fly."

It was decided that Brian would go first, then Carol, followed by Kees. She would have the most trustworthy of backcountry skiers to her front and back.

As soon as Brian shoved off the icy ridge, a lip over the chute, he was out of sight. Carol had always gained confidence when she could see Brian make his entry, but this time was different. He had disappeared.

The tension was almost unbearable. She paused—but it was now or never. The brief moment of hesitation seemed like an eternity, but there was no turning back. She had to take the plunge.

She made the steep drop into the ice-covered chute, knowing she would have to make seven or eight frighteningly quick turns to avoid crashing into the rocks on either side. She tried to set an edge but, in an instant, she was airborne, head over heels in full flight, descending more than two thousand feet at a speed close to eighty miles per hour. To try to comprehend the enormity of this fall, imagine falling off the top of a two-hundred-story building—or off the head of each of the four presidents, in succession, carved at Mt. Rushmore. It was a gigantic and terrifying accident, a fall into an unimaginable abyss.

Meeting Brian and Carol in Aspen some years later was also accidental. As Carol would say, it was a Bluebird day: clear skies, great weather, and perfect snow conditions. I was skiing alone and had stopped on the mountain at Bonnie's for a hot chocolate. With the hot cup in my hand, I walked down to the deck and tripped on the last step. I went sprawling and managed to spill the chocolate all over the deck and the table where the couple was sitting.

This kind stranger picked me up first, then the cup, and in just a few minutes brought a fresh cup of hot chocolate to the table. He said, "Don't worry, it was an accident. We all have accidents. My name is Brian, and this is my wife, Carol." We were the only ones on the deck and talked about how, after snowing all morning, the sun was now shining, and we had before us the delight of skiing in fresh powder on such a crystal-clear day.

At the time, I had no idea that I had just met two of the most extreme off-piste skiers who had backcountry skiing experiences I could only dream of. I learned about the book Carol Grant Sullivan had written about her unbelievable escape, rescue, survival, recovery, and rehabilitation after the more than two-thousand-foot fall. This horrendous event is fully covered in her gripping account, *Fall Line*. It is a must read for skiers and nonskiers alike; a captivating tribute to the human spirit.

Meeting Carol and Brian was accidental, but hardly incidental. It is a great pleasure to have met and to know this adventure-driven Canadian couple—all due to what turned out to be a happy (but not at all terrifying!) accident.

JUNIOR BOUNOUS

He is nearly two years older than I am but, like so many others younger than he, I proudly refer to him as "my Junior."

The nomination of Junior Bounous to the National Ski Hall of Fame stated that he was a "Pioneer in the American Ski Industry," and he has continued to be one of the most creative since he started skiing on barrel staves at the age of eight. His creativity, coupled with a strong desire to help others, has contributed to the excellence of so many great skiers and has earned him the appreciation of so many of us geriatric skiers.

Early on, he realized that he was more interested in the techniques of teaching people to ski than he was in skiing competitions. This realization determined a unique skiing career.

He started as an instructor in Alta, Utah, under the guidance of Alf Engen, known as Utah's Athlete of the Century. In 1948, at the age of twenty-three, Junior received his certification as a ski instructor, one of the youngest to do so at that time. From 1948 to 1958, he was Engen's professional assistant. As ski school director of California's Sugar Bowl Resort, a position he held starting in the 1958-59 season, he developed a program for children including the techniques for teaching them.

Junior moved back to Utah in the '60s and became a part owner of the Timp Haven Ski Resort. When it was bought by Robert Redford in 1969, the name was changed to the Sundance Ski Resort. However, Junior remained as the ski school director until he received an offer he couldn't refuse.

He was asked to map out and direct the construction of the now famous Snowbird Resort, which is next to Alta on Little Cottonwood Canyon, a short drive from Salt Lake City. When the resort opened in 1971, Junior was the first ski school director and twenty years later, in 1991, he went a step higher and became director of skiing. Long before, he had achieved the reputation of being the "instructor's instructor."

In his new position, he created a program for seniors called Silver Wings and offered a complimentary half-day program, "Junior's Seniors." I availed myself of both and learned so many wonderful techniques for skiing at an older age. Here's just one example.

Junior, noted for being one of the best powder skiers in the world, was also one of the best instructors in that art. His main admonition to his students for powder skiing was to keep your skis flat; if you set an edge in powder the snow will literally grab your ski and down you'll go. To get the feel of keeping your skis flat, Junior had a simple exercise. Simple? "Get on a beginner's slope and do 360s."

"360s?"

"Sure, start a turn and continue going around until you've made a complete circle and are in the same position you started in. It's easy if you keep your skis flat and pivot. If you set an edge, you'll fall."

Easy!

So off I went to Chicadee, the beginner's slope right alongside Snowbird's magnificent Cliff Lodge, in full view of many. "Easy! Just keep your skis flat." Flat? The only thing that was flat was me—flat on my back at least a dozen times, much to the amusement of the gallery. Then I stopped catching my edge. Finally, I got it! Well, not quite one hundred percent, but, at least now, when I fall in fresh powder, I know the reason why.

Junior Bounous is featured in more than ten Warren Miller films. When Miller was asked why he called upon Junior so often, his answer was, "Because he's better than anyone else!"

One of Warren Miller's films showed Junior with his skis on backward, skiing with his back facing downhill. He was one of the first to be filmed doing this, to the amazement of skiers the world over. No doubt his expertise in keeping his skis flat enabled him to accomplish this feat. Thankfully, he doesn't require us to do this in the Silver Wings program!

Junior Bounous' career is covered in the documentary film, "Bounouseabuse: 80 Junior Years." However, this kind man's only "abuse" is that his skiing and instructing abilities have surpassed and overshadowed all others.

MARTIN HECKELMAN

In the French Alps, there is no private ski instructor more in demand than Martin Heckelman. In particular, he has an immense following among the English.

I first met him at l'Hôtel Chamois d'Or in Val d'Isère. However, it was almost impossible to book a lesson with him, since year after year, he was monopolized by three English families staying at the hotel. As Marty worked with them, they constantly improved, and we enjoyed skiing with them.

When he started instructing the English families the parents were intermediate skiers and the children were beginners. Now they are all—yes, *all*—expert skiers with great skills in off-piste skiing

A few times I tagged along while they were taking lessons and, even though I had taken a ski instructor's course, I not only learned more about skiing but also more about instructing.

After telling Miguel so much about Val d'Isère, we finally booked a trip there. Before the trip, I visited Miguel in his home in Sao Paulo and noticed that he subscribed to *Ski Magazine*. The principal feature in that month's issue focused on Val d'Isère, with part of the article devoted to Martin Heckelman as a notable private ski instructor. Miguel and I discussed the article extensively; he was surprised that I knew Marty as a friend.

When we arrived at Val d'Isère, Miguel asked me to book a lesson for him with Marty, which I did, and they did very well together. My son Michael arrived, and I skied with him, but we also tagged along as we watched Miguel and Marty working on- and off-piste. It was January, but the snow conditions were excellent. It's difficult to find better skiing than in Val d'Isère.

The following week we went to Megève, probably the most upscale resort in the French Alps, comparable to St. Moritz in Switzerland. (Back in August, Miguel had booked the only three-star Michelin Restaurant in Megève for Michael's January birthday, explaining that he had to do it in August to be sure to get the reservation. August for a reservation in January? Well, it was a fantastic fifteen-course dinner.)

Megève, because of its relatively low altitude, is not noted for great ski conditions, but we hit it lucky. It snowed all night, and amazingly, we had over a foot of fresh powder the next day. It was heaven-sent! Even more amazing was how Miguel skied this deep powder. I couldn't believe my eyes. It was, indeed, a testimony to the excellence of Marty's ski instruction, to say nothing of the educability of Miguel. It was triumphant!

Marty started skiing in a Boy Scout camp on wooden skis that were donated by the U.S. Army's Tenth Mountain Division. The daily rental was fifty cents. After passing a ski instructor's course during his college days, he taught on weekends at Okemo and Jay Peak in Vermont. After graduating with a degree in electrical engineering, he worked at that for a few years before traveling to Europe, where he instructed at major ski resorts in Switzerland, Austria, France, and Italy. He also instructed in Chile, where he developed the "international parallel technique," which combined the best of the European and Chilean methods.

In France, after becoming a full time instructor in Megève, he discovered Val d'Isère and Tignes, with twenty-five thousand acres of abundant snow, hundreds of trails and lifts, and very few people. As Jean-Claude Killy had done before him, Marty made it his home.

Martin Heckelman is also known as Mr. Ski Tips and has written some of the finest books on the subject: *Step by Step Skiing Skills*; *The Hamlyn Guide to Skiing*; and most notably, *The New Guide to Skiing*, which covers the "new" language of Alpine skiing with Fat Boy skis, carving skis, cross skis, and extreme-shaped skis. He has also produced the *Ski Tips* video and DVD series that speaks that same language visually. Most recently he has produced a series of four *New Ski Tips APPS* for the iPhone, iPod, and iPod with video and audio combined.

The *Ski Tips* videos and DVDs together with the *New Ski Tips APPS* make up the most comprehensive ski instruction series ever made. Yet one has to question the word "tips" as it relates to Martin Heckelman and wonder if we are being exposed to just the "tip of the iceberg" of his vast skiing experience.

He recently said, "I get so much pleasure from teaching people to become safer, better skiers, and passing on my joy of the sport to them. I hope to keep skiing and teaching as long as my body holds up."

Finally, where does this most competent and illustrious ski instructor, who has taught so many English and other Europeans in the French Alps, come from?

Martin Heckelman was born and grew up in New York City, in the Borough of Brooklyn!

Martin Heckelman celebrating his life in Val d'Isère

DAVE POWERS

"Gravity is there all the time, but we only
feel it when we jump into its stream."

—Dave Powers

Dave is known as the Guru of Snowbird, with thirty-four years of skiing "the Bird" on an almost daily basis, giving him a unique knowledge of the resort. This Utah resort is unsurpassed in its proportions for skiers of all levels, with thirteen lifts serving 2,500 acres of meticulously groomed slopes and a fantastic array of off-piste possibilities. But there are very few who know all these possibilities as well as Guru Dave. He has worked on a rebel trail map showing nearly three hundred runs, most of which fall over three thousand feet from top to bottom. He has a name for every run, such as "Colossus," "Dutchy Draw," and "Kitty's Trees."

Dave's Web site, gurudavepowers.com, not only reports daily on snow conditions in all of Little Cottonwood Canyon (including Alta), but also points to where the best skiing is in Snowbird.

Growing up in Massachusetts, young Dave skied mainly in Vermont. His expertise in skiing is matched by his knowledge of philosophies from the mysticism of Rosicrucian to the beliefs of the New Age philosopher, Eckhart Tolle. Tolle's *The Power of Now*, a philosophy deeply conscious of the present moment, and Rudolph Steiner's *Moral Imagination*, which expresses the ability to discern and fulfill certain possibilities, are concepts that Dave has applied to his greatest love, skiing. These beliefs have given him the freedom to be creative and joyous, not only in skiing, but in life in general. He demonstrated this creativity when he persuaded his school, the University of Massachusetts, to establish a major course in comparative belief systems. This was, perhaps, his first step in becoming a guru.

His summer work, consisting of seven months as a leader of a road-paving crew, supports his five months of skiing. This has proven to be a well-chosen program, since there is little chance of both occupations overlapping!

Skiing with Guru Dave can be compared to attending a college of higher learning in the sport. He is a master of technique in skiing powder and in the most difficult of off-piste terrain. His knowledge of "the Bird's" territory can best be termed as professorial, with his warmth and sincerity shining through.

Angels have wings. Guru Dave can't quite be called an angel—but he does have wings. An airfoil, introduced by French skiers years ago, inspired him to design a pair of stubby wings for skiers to hold instead of ski poles. A surfboard shop cut the shapes out of foam, and Dave attached handles with duct tape. This was twenty years ago. Today, these three-ounce wings provide eight to ten pounds of lift, at a speed of thirty-five to forty-five miles per hour.

Guru Dave with his wings

If you're fortunate to meet Dave on the first tram of the day from the Snowbird Plaza to Hidden Peak, an eight-minute ride, you may have the ultimate guide to Snowbird's vast terrain. It might be days after a snowfall, but the guru will find obscure stashes of powder. If you have some trouble in your powder skiing technique, Dave will spot it and offer a solution. One time when I was skiing with him, he noticed what I was doing wrong and gave me a simple exercise using my index fingers. I was soon back in control.

In the year 2000, Snowbird expanded by opening Mineral Basin, a vast five hundred acres of skiable terrain. As a result, Dave's playground grew by nearly twenty-five per cent and provided unimaginable powder possibilities. Two years later, a high speed quad chairlift was installed, connecting Mineral Basin to Albion Basin in Alta. Now as an interconnected resort, Snowbird and Alta are a mind-boggling 4,700 acres. The world of Dave's skiing is now in the realm of a universe.

To Dave, skiing is a spiritual activity, and his thoughts are enhanced by a keen philosophical awareness. His words about Snowbird tell us much about him: "The Bird cannot be exaggerated, as the reality transcends exaggeration and is replete with legends and memories of all who have plumbed the depths of its incomparable essence. I am blessed!"

This extraordinary person is easy to identify, with his charcoal-colored hair and a walrus-like mustache. To know who he really is, is not that easy. According to him, he is "the foremost authority on nothing." That may be a sample of his humor, but is not the reality of him. He claims to be blessed, but those who have known Dave Powers over the years are the ones who are truly blessed!

VICENTE VERA

It was 1999, in late August, a good time to ski in Chile. I was joined at the Gran Hotel in Termas de Chillan by Miguel and Gisele, the two new friends from Brazil I had met in March at the Palace Hotel in St. Moritz. But regrettably, they had to return to Brazil earlier than expected, leaving me without skiing partners for two more days. I asked a member of the hotel staff if he could pair me up with a good skier, preferably someone about my age (then seventy-two). The following day, Vicente Vera was waiting for me in the ski room.

It was a case of good news and bad news. The good news was that I was fixed up with an Olympian ski racer. The bad news was that it was pouring rain. It was incomprehensible. August in South America is equivalent to February or March in North America. How could it be raining at this time of year, at this altitude?

Well, as we know it here in the North, it was spring skiing. During the winter, we ski on powder or packed powder. However, skiing in the spring presents a myriad of different conditions, one of which is pure delight: corn snow! The snow is softened by the warm weather during the day, but later, crystallizes into a sugarlike consistency. It is simply an enchanting ride to slide through these crystals, making skiing in fresh powder my second most desirable condition.

Most of the other spring conditions range from difficult to horrendous. There's granular or frozen granular, crust or breakable crust, hard-pack, ice, glare ice, and black ice. Most hateful are wet snow and pure slush. What we had at that time was something between those two.

Vicente was distraught and apologetic. "Normally, we have great snow at this time of the year. It doesn't rain, it snows. This is unexplainable." These daunting conditions did not deter me from skiing with this world-class skier. Following him was a learning experience that has stood me in good stead in the worst of conditions.

Vicente Vera, whose reputation in the ski areas of South America is remarkable, was a member of the Chilean team for the Winter Olympics at Cortina d'Ampezzo, Italy, in 1956; Squaw Valley, California, in 1960; and Innsbruck, Austria, in 1964.

Chile has some of the best ski resorts in South America, among which are the legendary Portillo and upscale Valle Nevado. Termas de Chillan is not upscale, but it is upcoming, blessed with nature's gift of wonderful hot springs. It also boasts of Las Tres Marias, with a ski run of thirteen kilometers (eight miles), the longest in South America.

When you go to Termas de Chillan, you will have hot springs, a casino, and a great South American ski area. Most importantly, you will have a three-time Olympian as a guide to show you the slopes. Vicente Vera holds sway at Termas de Chillan and conducts tours of the ski terrain twice a day. Skiing with an Olympian? It doesn't get much better anywhere.

THIERRY SCHOEN

We had just passed Berlin—Berlin, New York, on the way back from skiing at Killington, Vermont. I turned the driving over to Thierry as I was bushed after a weekend of trying to keep up with this world-class skier from France.

But now the New York State trooper caught up with us. "You were doing eighty in a fifty-mile zone. Let me see your driver's license and car registration." Pretending not to understand English, Thierry turned to Joan and asked, in French, "What's happening?" After she told him, he presented his international license to the trooper. When I proffered the car registration, I explained that the driver was accustomed to a speedometer showing kilometers per hour, and that he was aware that eighty kilometers was equivalent to fifty miles. The speedometer read eighty and, forgetting that it indicated miles, he converted that to fifty and thought he was within the speed limit. "Well, all right, but tell this guy he's driving an American car with a speedometer showing miles and not kilometers!" He let us go, and we continued on.

A little abashed by what he had done, "this guy" from France knew exactly what had happened. Thierry Schoen was here in the U.S. attending New York University for his master's degree in law. Coincidentally, this was not the only encounter he had had with New York police.

Thierry was one of four brothers who, together with their father Jean Pierre, were regulars at l'Hôtel Chamois d'Or in Val d'Isère where we spent so many of our Christmas holidays. The brothers—Frederic, Vincent and Pascal—were all highly rated ski racers. In addition to many titles, Thierry coached the ski team of the Racing Club de France and holds the esteemed title of Moniteur National with l'École du Ski Français to this day.

When Thierry came here in 1982 as a candidate for his master's degree, he initially stayed with us in Roslyn, Long Island. Because he wanted to get an idea of what skiing was like in the Eastern United States, we drove up to Hunter Mountain in the Catskills with Murray, a friend from my tennis club.

Thierry and I skied together and stopped for lunch. Murray did his own thing. and his lunch was the apple he carried with him. It was February 11, 1983, and on the way back, it started to snow heavily. And so began the Blizzard of 1983!

I suggested that we stop in Newburgh and sleep over as the driving was getting hazardous. They both said "No!" Murray, a dentist, had patients coming in the morning, and Thierry had an important exam. So on we went, Thierry doing the driving.

The way to Roslyn is across the George Washington Bridge to the Cross Bronx Expressway, then the Triboro Bridge to Long Island. Under normal conditions it's about a two-and-a-half hour drive. We left Hunter at 5:00 p.m. and reached the George Washington Bridge at about ten. Just as we crossed the bridge onto the Cross Bronx Expressway, traffic came to a complete stop. It was now eleven. We were finally able to crawl to an exit in the heart of the South Bronx, at that time a treacherous and dangerous section of the city. Weaving in and out through abandoned cars and trucks, Thierry slalomed through to reach the Triboro Bridge and onto the well-plowed Grand Central Parkway. *Voilà!* We had made it! Another thirty minutes and we would be home.

But no! The Grand Central hadn't been cleared all the way. A police car led us to a precinct station in Fresh Meadows. It was long past midnight. We hadn't eaten since noon, and Murray had had only an apple! There was a vending machine, but no one had quarters. We were each given a desk to sleep on.

This was Thierry's first encounter with the New York police.

Thierry received his masters in law at NYU and became a member of both the New York Bar and the Paris Bar. Realizing that his bit of skullduggery with the New York State trooper might jeopardize his standing with either bar, we asked Thierry to review this exposé, just in case the statute of limitations still applied!

However, there is no limitation to the high regard we have for Thierry and his family.

THE OLYMPICS

He nearly fell at the eleventh gate, and we were right there, so close to the course that, if he had fallen, we could have picked up the pieces—his skis, poles, goggles, that is.

But he didn't fall! That famously resilient and flamboyant Italian ski racer, Alberto Tomba, averted disaster, recovered and came from far behind in this second run of the giant slalom race at the 1992 Winter Olympics. We were on the Face de Bellevarde in Val d'Isère, where both the downhill and giant slalom races were being held.

The crowd roared when his time was announced, and we realized that Tomba had not only made a miraculous recovery, but had won the Olympic Giant Slalom Crown. Equally electrifying was the award ceremony that night when the high-powered Tomba (known as Tomba la Bomba by his fans) bowed to the cheering crowd and accepted the Olympic gold medal. It was almost as thrilling as the race itself. Face de Bellevarde was all aglow in shining lights and the Olympic torch. It was a moment to remember. And we were there.

Yes, we were there, as we were for seventeen Christmases at the Hôtel Chamois d'Or on a plateau at the base of Bellevarde. Joan and I and our boys, Jamie and Michael, learned and developed most of our skiing skills here in the ubiquitous French ski school, l'École du Ski Français. Michael's racing career blossomed on the lower part of the face of Bellevarde where so many races were run.

I was in the Top Ski program for advanced skiers in Val d'Isère created by two brothers, Jean and Pat Zimmer. A guide/instructor would take only three skiers for basically all off-piste skiing from 9:00 a.m. to 1:00 p.m. Jean called me one morning to tell me that one of our group was ill and, if I agreed, one of my sons could join us. Michael jumped at the chance.

After our session, Jean said that if I would leave Michael with him for four years, he would qualify for the Olympics. Olympics? I said, "He's only twelve years old. Is he that good?" Jean responded, "He has great potential." At the time, I didn't realize how costly that comment would become.

The following week, Michael and I entered a giant slalom race on a very difficult course near the base of Bellevarde. There were three pacesetters. Two of these pros didn't even finish this horrendous course. I didn't make it past the fourth gate, which required a nearly ninety-degree turn at top speed. Of the thirty-three racers, only three finished the course. Michael came in first.

Later that month, I took Michael to Catamount, a small New England ski area partly owned by one of my tennis club members. I asked him if their racing coach would give me an accurate appraisal of Michael's ability. After he ran a giant slalom course, the coach confirmed Jean Zimmer's assessment. However, I wasn't about to leave my son in France for four years with Jean! But this new development led to four years of high school at Vermont Academy and the Putney School, with dynamic participation on the ski teams of each.

Michael is a good skier. He still loves to race, even though he's now in his forties. He became fluent in French and spent several years in Paris after college. However, he never made the Olympics except for *being there* when Tomba la Bomba won the gold medal in giant slalom at the 1992 Winter Olympics.

RACING

Hardly anything helps to improve your skills in skiing more than racing. Developing racing techniques will serve to make your recreational skiing a great deal more enjoyable.

The key to successful racing is carving, which can enhance recreational skiing because it is less tiring than sliding or slipping. An early initiation of the turn *before* the fall line allows for setting the edges of the skis so that they will knife through the terrain without side slipping. In racing, side slipping will cause you to lose time; in recreational skiing it can create fatigue.

(Of course, all the other elements such as maintaining skis parallel, proper pivoting, pole planting, and rhythm, are essential.)

In 1968, *Ski Magazine* introduced NASTAR: National Standard Racing. Designed for citizen racing, this system handicaps according to age and sponsors a national competition to which each participating area sends its top racer. The winner's time establishes the National Standard. The time of each individual area's racer is figured as a percentage of the winner's time, thus establishing the handicap for the area. Added to that are handicaps for age. The courses are modified Giant Slalom courses and the average times are about thirty seconds.

Of course, the older you are the greater the handicap, and after some time, I accumulated a bucketful of bronze, silver and even some gold medals. Sometimes one of my boys would beat me down the course by a full second but, because of my handicap, I would win a gold and my son would only get a silver. Such are the rewards for getting older.

Michael and I also participated in some father and son races where the team was given a handicap of a tenth of a second for the number of years' difference between the father and son. I'm thirty-nine years older than Michael, which gave us a handicap of 3.9 seconds—an enormous handicap. However, we always came in second. Michael's father was neither fast enough nor old enough.

Probably the most embarrassing race I've been in was a combination ski race and tennis tournament for couples, introduced by the Vail (Colorado) racquet club. The first sixteen couples in the ski race would qualify for the mixed doubles tennis tournament. Joan and I are avid tennis players, but she had never raced before. Each couple raced on a parallel ski course. Husband and wife would start at the same time and their combined times would count toward qualifying for the tennis tournament. I told Joan to just ski carefully and finish the course.

We qualified for the tennis tournament but lost in the second round. Between the two of us, who was the one who was first down the race course? Every ski season, I am reminded that it wasn't me.

THE BIG ONE

The ski racing medal I am most proud of was the one I received in the first race I was ever in. It was in Les Menuires, one of the eight resorts that comprise Les Trois Vallées in France. The occasion was on our first visit to this mammoth ski complex which includes Courchevel, Meribel, Val Thorens, and La Tania.

It was our third year of skiing. Jamie, Michael, and I worked our way up to Class One in l'École du Ski Français; the next and highest level would be the Competition Class. Our instructor had put us through a rigorous workout that morning. Toward the end of the session, he brought us to the top of a race course where we were given numbered bibs and told we were in a race. We had never raced before!

The race was not only for our group; there were about sixty skiers altogether. It was sprung on us so abruptly that there wasn't any time to get nervous, but yes, I *was* nervous. It was a giant slalom course, and the race was designated *la Flèche* (the arrow).

When I finished the course and my time was announced on the loudspeaker, one of the members of our group from Paris threw his arms around me and screamed, "You won the big one! You won the big one!" He thought I had won the gold medal, but he had heard the numbers from the loudspeaker wrong. I didn't win the big one, the gold. But I *did* win the bronze.

Why was this accomplishment more meaningful than any other? It wasn't age-handicapped. I was racing on even terms with all the other skiers.

Michael won the *Flèchette*, the medal a step below the bronze. Jamie caught a tip on one of the gates and went down, but he doggedly got back on his skis, climbed back to the entry of the gate, and finished the course. This was the most significant part of the entire day. He didn't quit and that attitude characterizes him to this day. I was proud of my bronze medal and Michael's Flèchette, but I will always remember with pride how Jamie skied that race.

Joan was in the crowd at the top of the course. That night she told me that when I started, someone yelled, "Look at that old man go!" I was all of forty-eight years old.

Jamie conquering the Morteratsch Glacier, years later

PORTILLO, HEIDI, A SLINGSHOT,
AND A SUNDAY DRIVER

It's August 1999. Where can you ski? Where is there snow? Perhaps you should take a cruise instead? Is there a way to do both? Well, nearly.

For more than fifty years, Portillo, South America's premier ski resort, has been known internationally for its isolated setting in a sea of white. It's not the Atlantic or the Pacific, but a sea of powder snow in the majestic Andes.

Self-contained, Portillo has no villages, towns, or cities nearby. It is like a cruise ship nestled in the magnificent Andes Mountains of Chile. Ski racing teams from around the world come there to practice for the Olympics and world championships. This "cruise ship's" crew also hosts all those skiers from the Northern Hemisphere who need their summer "fix" of snow skiing.

In addition to its many chairlifts, Portillo has four unique *Va et Vient* (French for Come and Go) lifts, which I've never seen anywhere else. The threat of occasional avalanches that could flatten a major lift prompted the Poma Company to create these specially designed lifts for Portillo. Pulleys from the top take five skiers up the slope "sitting" side by side on Poma discs suspended from a bar. The initial pull is like a slingshot as you're catapulted up the hill. At first, it's quite jarring and you hate it, but after a few times you begin to love it; it's like water-skiing uphill. *Water-skiing?* Well, as mentioned above, here's a way to take a cruise while skiing!

Heidi Knaus, a prominent mainstay of the ski school at the Palace Hotel in St. Moritz, has equal notability at the ski school in Portillo and elsewhere. She has instructed in Canada and the United States, including nine years in Aspen, with the highest certifications. This Swiss charmer has turned many a beginner into an intermediate skier in very little time . . . and on three continents!

Though I knew Heidi for many years in St. Moritz, we never skied together; she was always in great demand at the Palace and fully booked. However, when I arrived in Portillo she greeted me with "Stanley! I'm not booked this week, and we can ski together!" It was an offer I couldn't refuse and a welcome I will never forget.

It snowed and snowed. Not only was it mind-boggling to be skiing in deep powder snow in the middle of August, but skiing with Heidi was special. Though it was not her intention to instruct me, following her lead was a great experience. She kept urging me on, "Ski more down the fall line; you ski like a Sunday Driver."

On the last day, Heidi took me to the top of a giant slalom course and insisted that I do the race. I said, "You want me to race at my age?" (I was then seventy-two.) "Why not! But don't ski like a Sunday Driver—you have to ATTACK, ATTACK, ATTACK!" ATTACK? I would be happy to just finish the course! Which I did, and was rewarded with a handshake from one of the officials; a bit of a triumph.

That night was the farewell celebration and the presentation of various awards. Heidi embellished the proceedings with a display of another of her talents, expertise on the concertina. Astonishingly, I was called to the podium where I was handed a large silver trophy. "Congratulations! You won the Sol de Portillo Giant Slalom race!" Incredulously, I said, "I won the race? Come on!"

"Yes, you did, you won it in your category." I decided not to ask how many were in my category. Most likely, I was the fastest in my group as well as the slowest. I guess it's the only time that the Sol de Portillo has been won by a Sunday Driver.

Winning the Portillo de Sol race!

Receiving the award, as Heidi plays a musical tribute

"WE KILLED HIM!"

It started in August 1995 in Las Leñas near Mendoza, one of the two ski resorts I've been to in Argentina; the other is Bariloche.

Las Leñas, with an elevation of 11,253 feet, is one of the most desirable ski resorts in South America. There were snowfalls almost every day providing some of the best powder skiing ever.

We enjoyed great companionship with members of the Miami Ski Club staying at the same hotel. Although we weren't registered with their group, they invited us to all their cocktail parties. Après-skiing with them was delightful. Even though we live in New York, we decided to join the Miami Ski Club. Why not? The largest ski club in the U.S. just became a little larger.

The following February, we joined the club on a trip to Purgatory and Telluride in Colorado. (Purgatory is now referred to as Durango Mountain Resort. Whatever! Under either name it is a helluva ski resort.) A luncheon was scheduled at the top of Telluride at Giuseppi's, a restaurant purported to be the highest (at an altitude of 11,890 feet) in the American Rockies. (Well, it may be the highest in the Rockies, but it can't really be classified as a restaurant: it's self-service!)

It was one of those gloriously warm, sunny days that occur so often in the Rockies during midwinter. There was no need for a ski jacket; a sweater over a turtle-neck was all that was necessary. We carried our food out to one of two very long bench-type tables in the brilliant sunshine. Alas, in about twenty minutes all these Floridians finished their lunch and got up to go skiing. I said, "Sorry, guys, I usually take at least an hour for lunch; I learned to ski in Europe."

There I was, alone, when, at the other table, five women greeted another five as they sat down. "I'm Nancy," "I'm Helen," "I'm JoAnn," "I'm Judy," and "I'm Pamela." I got a big laugh when I raised my arm and declared, "I'm Stanley." Pamela, who spoke with a British accent and was an extremely good-looking woman, reminded me of the actress who starred with Robert Mitchum in *War and Remembrance*. When I asked her if she was, she said no, she wasn't, "but I know whom you mean." Obviously, I was not the only one who had mistaken her for Jane Seymour.

After a short while, Pamela and Judy got up and turned to me. "Are you alone? Would you like to ski with us?" How could I refuse? Judy pulled me aside, and cautioned: "You don't know what you've gotten yourself into. Pamela King was a ski instructor in New Zealand, and she's wild!"

Yes, she was! She took me on every mogul run in Telluride including the infamous "Plunge," a world-renowned bump run. After a weak complaint that I needed a gentler slope, she took me on "The Milk Run." *Milk!* It was almost my undoing. I asked her if she was still a ski instructor, and she said that she was now selling real estate, and that she would like to ski with me again but had to go to work.

The next day, I was on a chairlift with another real estate agent and mentioned that I had skied with Pamela King the day before. "You skied with Pamela King? She's wild!" I said, "Yes, but she's also beautiful." And that's when I learned that she was once Miss New Zealand and came close to becoming Miss World.

It was a memorable first visit to Telluride. The subject of Miss New Zealand came up again several weeks later and several thousand miles away.

It was now March and we flew into Zurich, picked up a car, and joined a group in Zell am Ziller, Austria, led by the tour operator Adventures on Skis. The Zillertal has some of the finest ski areas in Austria (undiscovered by most American skiers), including Hintertux, the magnificent glacier, and Gerlos, a broad powder arena. In the same area is Mayrhofen, a favorite of the Brits, and where we were introduced to the Zillertal skiing at Fügen and Hochfügen.

We became friendly with an attractive young couple from Petaluma, California, and skied and dined with them most of the time. We offered to drive them to Kitzbühel, less than an hour away. One of the oldest and most famous of Austrian ski areas, Kitzbühel is the home of the Hahnenkamm Olympic downhill run and something to talk about if you ski it.

On the way, JoAnn mentioned that they had a home in Telluride and would be very happy to have us as guests. "Telluride? Why we were just there a few weeks ago!" I related the incident at Giuseppi's, and she screamed, "You're Stanley!" Somewhat puzzled, I said, "JoAnn, of course

I'm Stanley. We've been skiing together all week." "No, I mean that I was there at that table when you raised your arm and shouted, "I'm Stanley." What a coincidence.

She then said, "You may not have realized that it was Women's Week in Telluride. After skiing each day we would get together at a bar. Pamela and Judy came into the bar that day, pumped their fists in the air, and triumphantly declared. 'We killed him!'"

FOOTNOTE: In my next life, it would give me great pleasure to be such a victim while skiing bumps with Miss New Zealand in Telluride, Colorado.

VAL D'ISÈRE / TIGNES
AND L'ESPACE KILLY

If you have never skied in Europe and were to ask for my recommendation as to where to go (aware that I've skied over fifty European resorts), I wouldn't hesitate to say, "Zermatt, Switzerland." But when I am asked where in the Alps is the *best skiing*, without hesitation, I reply, "Val d'Isère, France." Why the difference? It's a combination of history, landscape, and terrain.

Zermatt's history centers around the Matterhorn, whose legendary challenge to mountain climbers preceded its eventual emergence as one of the world's great ski resorts. Much of its history is documented on the gravestones in the Zermatt cemetery. They tell the tales of those defeated by the horrendous climb to reach the summit of this awesome mountain, as well as of those who fell while making the equally treacherous descent to the base.

Val d'Isère's history is also not without tragedy, mainly of death from avalanches. The most tragic of these events occurred on February 10, 1970, when an avalanche racing at 120 mph swept through the village in waves up to one thousand yards wide. It smashed into a youth hostel killing thirty-nine students from Belgium, France, and Germany while they were having breakfast. The following day, at Bourg-Saint-Maurice, another avalanche swept away vehicles evacuating survivors. Yet these events, though horrific, are not the history for which this area is known.

Val d'Isère's history celebrates the dominance in the world of ski racing in the 1960s of its native son, Jean-Claude Killy.

Killy captured gold medals in all three disciplines (downhill, slalom, and giant slalom) during the 1968 Winter Olympics in Grenoble. It was a sensational achievement that stands alone in the history of Olympic ski racing. As a result, Val d'Isère, and the vast ski region of Tignes to which it is linked, is now known as l'Espace Killy (Killy's Space).

As for landscape, there is no place I know of in the Alps that can rival Zermatt, blessed with the Matterhorn and so many other great peaks such as Stockhorn, Weisshorn, and Monte Rosa.

L'Espace Killy, however, can be considered a close second, with Tête de Solaise, Col d'Iseran, Bellevarde, La Grande Motte, and the peaks surrounding Tignes. On a clear day the Italian side of Mont Blanc (at Cormayeur) is visible. There is also another of nature's enchantments, the Aguille Percée (Eye of the Needle) which pierces the sky above Tignes les Boisses. It takes a bit of climbing, but it's one of skiing's best photo ops.

So how do Val d'Isère, Tignes, and l'Espace Killy excel? Why are they considered to be the best area for skiing in the Alps, perhaps in the world? It's the skiing terrain!

Having skied in most of the major resorts in the United States, Canada, and Europe, as well as in South America and New Zealand, I don't know of any other terrain that compares with l'Espace Killy. I've skied there twenty times and have probably asked at least one hundred fellow skiers if they know of another area that compares with it. No one I asked could think of one.

Val d'Isère and Tignes are in the Tarentaise Valley of the Haute Savoie, a valley with some of the greatest ski resorts in the Alps. It includes La Plagne, Les Arcs, and Les Trois Vallées which together form a complex of eight interconnected resorts: Brides-les-Bains, Courchevel, Meribel-Mottaret, Les Menuires, St. Martin de Belleville, Orelle, La Tania and Val Thorens. Two hundred ski lifts interconnect them, providing an amazing safari.

So what makes l'Espace Killy, Val d'Isère and Tignes the 25-carat diamond among all these jewels of the skiing world?

Val d'Isère itself is known for its vast off-piste skiing which allows for powder skiing at almost every level. Unlike most ski areas in the United States, the powder lasts for many days after a snowfall because of a tremendous arena of untouched powder.

Though most off-piste skiing is meant for more experienced skiers, there are many possibilities for intermediates. One such run is the Tour de Charvet which encircles Bellevarde and offers both a great variety of terrain and unusual views, quite different from other snowscapes in Val d'Isère. It can be handled by most intermediates when the snow is good. However, there is always the threat of avalanche as there is in most off-piste areas. It is best to have a guide who is knowledgeable of the terrain and avalanche hazards.

Val d'Isère's reputation as best for advanced and expert skiers is well deserved. For beginners and intermediates, however, the entire complex of l'Espace Killy has ski terrain that is equally desirable. The groomed pistes, green for beginners, blue for intermediates, red for advanced, offer a rainbow of unending possibilities. The black pistes for experts are, of course, not in the rainbow and are extremely challenging.

A short walk from the center of Val d'Isère village brings you to the valley formed by the two principal mountains, Solaise on the left (south) and Bellevarde on the right (north). There is a myriad of ski lifts, cable cars, gondolas, and chairlifts, as well as an underground funicular at La Daille to bring skiers and nonskiers to the levels where lunch is served and skiing begins.

The runs down the face of these mountains vary from difficult to *very* difficult. The main feature of the face of Solaise is the moguls—bumps, *bumps,* and BUMPS! One must be a good skier to be able to handle this with any finesse.

The face of Bellevarde, which was the site of the downhill and giant slalom, super G, and combined races in the 1992 Olympics, presents an additional challenge of steep sections with some hairpin turns.

Yet as with so much of the Alps, the tops of the mountains and the glaciers are relatively flat. The ski slopes have moderate inclines which are excellent for teaching beginners and quite enjoyable for intermediate cruising. In this respect, the summits of both Solaise and Bellevarde are among the best in the Alps. Add the infinite amount of similar slopes in the Tignes region and it is difficult to find anything comparable.

South of Solaise is Le Fornet, yet another vast ski area, accessible by a cable car. More interesting than *le Train Rouge*, which first takes you to the cable car, are the ways to reach Le Fornet on skis from the top of Solaise. There is a tunnel that goes through the high ridge separating the two areas, or you can ski to a chairlift that goes up and over the ridge. Coincidentally, there is another chairlift on that side that goes down and then up, instead of the reverse. So skiing, like most other endeavors, has its ups and downs.

The principal feature of Le Fornet is the Glacier Pissaillas. This is only partially groomed, allowing multiple paths of off-piste skiing through untouched powder. Steeper runs are near Signal d'Iseran. The Signal drag lift takes you to two off-piste routes, L'Épaule and Vallon du Petit Signal. Be prepared for bumps as well as the powder.

From Val d'Isère village, Bellevarde is to the north. The skiing terrain at the top can be reached either by a gondola from the valley, or by the funicular near La Daille that runs through the mountain and carries 250 skiers to the top in just four minutes—a remarkable engineering feat. Cruising runs abound at the top of Bellevarde for the joy and pleasure of intermediate and advanced skiers. The runs back down to La Daille are somewhat more difficult but are worth the effort if you're interested in reaching some extraordinary restaurants.

The Tammeuse lifts from the top of La Daille will take you to Tovière, a higher peak. The entire region of Tignes is now in sight and accessible by several routes.

A major feature of Tignes is La Grande Motte, the mountain with the highest peak in l'Espace Killy. It is accessed from the village of Val Claret by still another engineering marvel, a funicular through the mountain and then a cable car to the top. Skiing down is cruising, more of a high speed kind, and then a choice of a challenging mogul run, steep off-piste skiing, or more gentle cruising which will take you back to Bellevarde by a lift from the Col de Fresse.

If you ski to the modern, purpose-built village of Lac de Tignes from Tovière you will pass some excellent beginner terrain. Then, across the road, you will have a truly mountainous array of intermediate, advanced, and expert runs. It is the major part of the Tignes skiing region. The most adventurous section includes the runs down to Tignes les Brévières, the very bottom of the entire l'Espace Killy, with routes for both experts and intermediates. You will ski past Tignes les Boisses in view of a hydroelectric dam that was built after WW II for desperately needed electricity.

It was a great achievement for French engineering and for the good of France, but it meant that the old village of Tignes had to be drowned. The dam was completed and the village submerged in 1952. Once every ten years Lac du Chevril, the lake behind the dam, is drained for maintenance work and the remains of the old village become visible. If you can't wait for this event, then continue on to the lowest part of l'Espace Killy, Tignes les Brévières.

Lunch at any number of restaurants in Tignes les Brévières is a well earned treat. Getting back to Val d'Isère includes another mind-boggling diversity of ski terrain, all of which makes the skiing in l'Espace Killy the *very best* in the Alps.

A NIGHT TO REMEMBER

The center of the 1992 Winter Olympics in France was Albertville. However, the downhill, giant slalom, super G, and combined races were on Bellevarde in Val d'Isère. The Olympic torch was situated about two hundred yards above the base of the mountain and above the Chamois d'Or, the hotel that was our family Christmas holiday abode for seventeen years. Located on a small plateau just above the base of Bellevarde, the Chamois d'Or is a ten-minute walk to the center of Val d'Isère.

As we returned to the hotel one night, walking past the cable car station at the base of Solaise, it was delightful to look across the valley and see the Olympic torch glowing on Bellevarde, forming a glimmering halo on the snow above the hotel. A bright moon shone down and reflected on the creek running through the valley. Though it was a clear, starry night, there were still some snow flurries as we walked across the small bridge and up the path to the Chamois d' Or.

We looked up and saw the dancing flames emerging from the Olympic torch as the descending snowflakes flickered and did their own dance in the moonlight. It was very quiet; the silence created its own music, a touch of fantasy. It seemed miraculous.

As we came to the door of the hotel, we turned and looked across the valley toward Solaise and the sky above. And there in the sky was an old friend that we had seen on starry nights for all those years—the mythological hunter, Orion, with the stars forming his belt and sword.

It was a night to remember! Even today, whenever I see this constellation, no matter where I am, in my mind I'm back in Val d'Isère in 1992.

Michael above the finish line of the Grand Slalom on Bellevarde, 1992 Olympics

The author, with the downhill course in the background on Bellevarde, 1992 Olympics

ALBERT EINSTEIN
AND WARREN MILLER

What does meeting Albert Einstein, perhaps the greatest scientist of the twentieth century, have to do with Warren Miller, an icon of the skiing world? The story starts in the year 1934.

Burnet Hershey (my Uncle Jack), in his role as a war correspondent, wrote and produced a documentary film condemning the munitions industry during the First World War. The film, *Dealers in Death*, opened in New York at the Criterion Theater with all of the Hirsch family in attendance.

In the lobby after the screening, Uncle Jack took me by the arm and brought me over to meet his close friend, Albert Einstein. I was not quite eight years old and didn't have any awareness of this extraordinary scientist. I thought I might have heard his name somewhere, but . . . ?

Some sixty-five years later, on the way to Alaska for a fishing trip, I stopped in Seattle to visit with friends, Howard and Carol Wright. (Howard was the builder of the Seattle Space Needle.) After a night at their beautiful home on Lake Washington, we flew to Orcas Island on Puget Sound in their float plane to their magnificent summer complex. After breakfast the following morning, Howard, knowing I was a skier, asked me if I would like to meet his neighbor, Warren Miller.

Warren Miller? By all means! Meeting Warren Miller, this icon of the skiing world . . . now, this would be something to remember . . . truly something to *really* be thrilled about!

Miller's career is legendary. He started as a ski instructor in Sun Valley where he was selected to be a player in an early film about skiing. After the shooting of the film, the producer persuaded him to explore a film-making career. It was a momentous life-changing decision.

MEMOIRS OF A GERIATRIC SKI BUM

Throughout the years, he has become the dominant figure in the production of skiing films, mainly those focusing on the dangerous and exciting world of extreme skiing. His reputation as a cinematic artist is well-earned and his worldwide audiences have eagerly awaited each of his newly released films.

Miller now writes an excellent monthly column for *Ski Magazine*. Very often, after reading one of his articles, I say to myself, "I wish I had said that." It's a combination of adventure, wisdom, and attitude, as he relates his own "love affair" with skiing. For Warren, it's been a life-long romance.

We discussed many things about skiing that morning. He asked me if I had tried the new powder skis, referring to the "Fat Boys." These were made extremely wide so they would float near the top of, and not sink deep into, the powder. It's the same technology for snowboards. I said, "Yes, but I felt like I was cheating." He replied, "Listen, Stanley, at our age we need all the help we can get."

How true that statement is! It's a thought that comes to mind, not only in skiing, but in many other physical and even some mental activities I experience at the age of eighty-four. However, that bit of wisdom—to take all the help we can get—applies more readily to skiing, as demonstrated in the following circumstances:

One example is how the 70+ Ski Club overnights in Denver before going to Vail, Steamboat, Aspen, or any of the other high altitude resorts in the Rockies. That overnight stop in mile-high Denver helps skiers get accustomed to the lower oxygen levels they will experience at the higher altitudes.

While skiing, frequent stops for coffee or hot chocolate allow for adequate pacing and the saving of energy.

There's another problem regarding frequent stops—for older men. When going to an area new to them, they scope out where the restrooms are. However, it's much more helpful and convenient to find a well-situated tree and eliminate the necessity of getting out and back into skis. (Sorry, ladies—I know it's not as easy for you!)

When there's a choice of ski lifts, it's best for older skiers to select a chairlift or gondola rather than a cable car; sitting rather than standing helps to conserve energy!

If you want to last longer throughout the day, stay on the groomed slopes. If you *do* get into deep powder, try to have a younger and/or stronger skier behind you. If you fall in powder, getting up and back into skis is a bummer. It's always good to have a helping hand. Yes, we need all the help we can get!

Comparing meeting Warren Miller to the meeting of Albert Einstein may be somewhat of a stretch. But in a way, Warren Miller has been as important to the world of skiing as Albert Einstein has been to the scientific world.

We really don't know if Einstein ever skied. If not a skier, the fact that this nuclear scientist might have been a designer of skis is a distinct possibility. After all, the powder skis that Warren Miller referred to, the Fat Boys, are manufactured by a firm whose name is—"Atomic"!

ROTAIR, ENGELBERG, AND LUZERN

There are only three rotating cable cars in the entire world and only one—the Rotair in Engelberg, Switzerland—that services a ski resort. The Rotair has the distinction of being the very first rotating cable car ever, and without realizing it at the time, I rode it in its first month of operation.

The other two are in Palm Springs, California, offering views of Mount San Jacinto's Chino Canyon, and the Table Mountain Aerial Cableway in South Africa with views of Cape Town and the Atlantic Ocean.

The Rotair climbed to the top of Titlis Mountain as I marveled at views of the Swiss Alps that changed as the car rotated. The floor of the car, in the shape of a hockey puck, made the rotating movement within the frame of panoramic windows encircling the cable car. The Rotair is the third of three aerial cable lifts which begin with an enclosed gondola from the valley floor of Engelberg, carrying you to another cable car which takes you to the station where you board the Rotair. The entire ride, with its two stops, takes about forty minutes. In 1927, the *Engelberg Gazette* described the original cable car ride as follows: "Down below, the abyss; above, the whisper of the cable. You soar into the deep blue skies as if whisked by winds."

Engelberg, "The Mountain of Angels," and its environs form the largest ski region in central Switzerland and boasts the longest ski run in the Alps: twenty-six kilometers (over sixteen miles), from the top of Mt. Titlis to the valley. World Cup ski jump competitions are held yearly on Mt. Titlis the weekend before Christmas.

The Ice Flyer, a special chairlift at the top, presents close views of the Titlis glacier and its crevasses and brings you to the Restaurant Stubli on the Sun Terrace with equally spectacular sights. Below the summit is the Glacier Cave with ice tunnels leading into a frozen world. It is a favorite tourist attraction and filming opportunity.

The north-facing Titlis glacier is a paradise for deep powder skiers, with consistent snows and seldom touched terrain.

Just an hour away from Engelberg is Luzern, the "City of Lights," considered the fifth most popular tourist destination in the world. It is situated next to Lake Luzern and straddles the Reuss River. Among its many tourist attractions are the fourteenth century Chapel Bridge with its unique octagonal tower, and Mt. Pilatus, ascended by cog- and cableways, and snow-covered at the summit even in August.

The Luzern Festival Orchestra is another major attraction, as are the Luzern Blues Festival, the Festival Rose d'Or and many carnival celebrations.

Legend has it that an angel with a light guided the first settlers to Luzern. Together with Engelberg and the Rotair, its ethereal rotating cable car, a visit to this area in central Switzerland is simply *heavenly!*

The author riding the Rotair in its first month of operation

INTERLAKEN, GSTAAD, AND 007

The Bernese Oberland in the middle of Switzerland is the highest region of the Canton of Berne. It is the home of some of the most spectacular ski resorts in the Alps.

Interlaken (Between the Lakes) is in the center of the region. Situated between Lake Thun and Lake Brienz, it is one of the oldest and still one of the most popular tourist resorts in Switzerland. About an hour's drive from Bern, the country's capital, is a network of 213 kilometers (133 miles) of trails on a vast expanse of ski slopes. Some of the most famous summits in the Alps, the Jungfrau, the Eiger and Schilthorn, embrace these slopes and form valleys which are picture-postcard beautiful. Ascending the Jungfrau by train provides you with one of the most scenic journeys by rail on the planet.

The Lauterbrunnen Valley provides access to the three major ski resorts of the Jungfrau Region. The best-known is Grindelwald, about thirty minutes by car or train from Interlaken. The first chairlift in Switzerland was installed on the ski area called *First* (meaning "peak") and is accessed from one side of the village; the train station is at the other side. A train will take you to Mannlichen where, at the top, is a flat plateau known as the Beach, with about fifty beach chairs there for sunbathing.

Another stop on the train is Kleine Scheidegg, a ski area that saddles the two resorts of Grindelwald and Wengen. In the area is the longest men's downhill race on the World Cup Circuit, the Lauberhorn. Racers complete the run in about two minutes. Recreational skiers? Some negotiate the course in less than an hour.

From the Lauterbrunnen Valley, a cable car or cog railway brings you to the Mürren/Schilthorn ski area. Mürren, a tiny, quaint village, provided a perfect setting for the James Bond movie, *On Her Majesty's Secret Service*. Overlooking Mürren at the top of Schilthorn is the revolving restaurant

Piz Gloria, which makes a complete revolution in fifty-five minutes and proudly displays "007" across the spread of its windows. The restaurant presents a magnificent panorama of the Bernese Alps and views that reach as far as Mont Blanc in France.

The Schilthorn peak is reached by a series of cable cars from the valley and the village of Mürren which, like Wengen, is car-free. To ski down from Piz Gloria requires a healthy amount of verve. The first fifty yards from the top are treacherously steep; I skied it only once, and it was hair-raising. It's the famous black run featured in the aforementioned Bond film.

Skiing the Mürren/Schilthorn slopes is for strong intermediates, advanced, and expert, not for beginners. Fortunately, the cable car that brings you up to the Piz Gloria also goes the other way. You can actually make the round trip from Mürren without skis. Many ski areas are featured in James Bond movies, but none reflects the allure of Bond more than tiny Mürren.

Gstaad is in the western part of the Bernese Oberland and about forty-five miles (seventy kilometers) from Interlaken. The drive from Interlaken to Gstaad takes less than an hour and a half; there is also a railway link.

If the Jungfrau Region and Interlaken together can be considered a Swiss gem, then Gstaad might be called a crown jewel. It is truly royal, one of the most exclusive resorts in the world, and one of the largest in the Alps.

This romantic mountain village nestled in the Alps is the Swiss resort of fairy tales. The most prominent feature is a picturesque castle that sits on a hill overlooking the village. At night, this Gstaad Palace is illuminated by a string of pearls, a necklace of spotlights. This car-free village's charm is enhanced by other luxurious hotels and a promenade of numerous highly exclusive shops and restaurants.

Attending the high society nightlife events are celebrities from all corners of the world. Famous residents have included the actresses Julie Andrews, Elizabeth Taylor, and Jeanne Moreau, as well as the director Roman Polanski and the financier George Soros. In the past, regular visitors included the violinist Yehudi Menuhin, the movie star David Niven, former British Prime Minister Margaret Thatcher, Prince Rainier and Princess Grace of Monaco, HRH Prince Charles of Great Britain, and King Juan Carlos and Queen Sofia of Spain.

Switzerland is a multicultural nation, with French and German representing the largest ethnicities. The dividing line between these two distinct parts of the country is close to Gstaad. French-speaking Rougemont is just a few miles away as are the ski areas Château d-Oex and Les Diableret.

If you ever get to Rougement, scope out Café du Cerf for the best Raclette you will ever have.

The Gstaad "Super Ski Region" is immense. It is best to have a car to reach the various ski areas, though all are accessible by bus or train. Minutes from the center of Gstaad are the areas of Wispile, Wasserngrat, and Eggli, which are not interconnected. However, Eggli is interconnected with La Vidamanette which leads you to Rougement. Skiing from Gstaad to Rougement and back is a delightful all-day affair, especially if you stop for lunch in Rougement.

A few minutes from the village of Saanen (close to Gstaad), the road leads to Schonried and the ski areas of Rellerli, Horneggli, and Saanenmöser. Horneggli and Saanenmöser are interconnected and you can go still farther from Saanenmoser to Zweisimmen, another delightful all day of skiing.

A drive of about thirty-five minutes from Gstaad brings you to Lenk, which is linked to Adelboden. The two combined form another vast ski area more than equal to either of those described above. After my one and only visit to this combo, I barely made the cable car to get me back to my car and return to the Gstaad Palace.

The Gstaad Palace, built in 1913, has earned its reputation for refined hospitality to a most discerning international clientele. I have stayed there quite often due to their holding a backgammon tournament the week before the one in St. Moritz. It is as elegant as the Palace Hotel in St. Moritz, but its decor is more akin to a hunting lodge than a ski lodge.

Notably, there have been only two lodges or hotels that I have visited in all of ski-dom that have dining rooms with live music and a dance floor—the Sun Valley Lodge in Idaho and the Gstaad Palace. The attraction of the backgammon tournament was only second to the heavenly dining and dancing at the Gstaad Palace.

The Eagle Ski Club at the top of Wasserngrat caters to high society, the hoi polloi, and, yes, *le jet set*. There is a three-year wait to obtain membership; gaining membership is a cause for celebration. Membership costs only about $40,000, a small price to pay for having lunch in a restaurant with film stars such as Richard Burton, Liz Taylor, or Peter Sellers. It is also not uncommon to have four or five kings, queens, or princes in the restaurant at the same time. This is not my element, but my friends Lyn and Pat Berger were members and gracious hosts who invited me there for lunch several times. More importantly, they arranged for me to have skiing partners during my stay in Gstaad.

Probably the most prominent member of the Eagle Club at the time I was there was Roger Moore, responsible for so many fascinating ski scenes in James Bond movies. His skiing as "007" in the films *The Spy Who Loved Me* and *A View to Kill* is most memorable.

However, one of the best James Bond movies with skiing scenes is also a message to those reading this book. The movie is *For Your Eyes Only*. For those perusing these pages, this book is most definitely *not* for your eyes only!

CHINA TO SIBERIA TO MONGOLIA—
AND THEN FOREVER

How does one travel to China, Siberia, and Mongolia without leaving America? Just go to Vail Ski Resort in Colorado.

There are three major sectors of this famous resort: the Frontside, the Back Bowls, and Blue Sky Basin. Since they are interconnected, you can ski them all without taking off your skis. Three major lifts will access the Frontside with a vast array of beginner, intermediate, and expert terrain consisting of green, blue and black runs. Chairlift number 4 or number 11 will bring you to the ridge that forms the top of Frontside. From there, you enter the Back Bowls.

In ski parlance, a bowl is a formation of semicircular opposing mountains that join to form a valley. The shape of this formation clearly resembles a bowl.

A traverse on Poppyfields West will lead you to China—China Bowl, the most gentle of all the Back Bowls. Much of it is groomed, and the runs are a joy for intermediate skiers.

At the bottom, the Poppyfields run will bring you to the Orient Express chairlift. From the top of Orient, you go farther east on Silk Road which will bring you to Siberia—Siberia Bowl. Gorky Park, Red Square, Rasputin's Revenge, and Bolshoi Ballroom are all powder and all black runs that will bring you back to the Orient Express lift.

Going east on Silk Road, you bypass Siberia and arrive in Mongolia. There you have a choice of bowls—Inner or Outer Mongolia. You are now in serious expert terrain of deep powder and the steeps. You might call them Super Bowls!

The runs bring you back to the Orient Express, returning to Silk Road, which then encircles Outer Mongolia and heads back west to the Skyline

Express lift. It takes you out of the Orient and the Back Bowls into Blue Sky Basin.

There are two bowls in Blue Sky Basin: Pete's and Earl's, each serviced by express quad chairlifts. From the top of Earl's Express, there are several friendly runs that will take you back to the Silk Road. The most popular is Cloud 9, with many choices through gladed areas of untouched champagne powder after a snowfall.

The top of Pete's Express is 11,570 feet, the highest point in Vail. The blue runs Grand Review and Star join Cloud 9 and bring you to the Tea Cup Express lift and the Tea Cup Bowl. Take it up and ski down Sun Up Bowl to High Noon lift, which allows you to traverse to Game Creek Bowl or ski down Sun Down Bowl.

It seems there are more bowls in Vail than in a soup kitchen.

History dictates that your first run down Sun Down Bowl is Forever, which brings us to the exhilarating story of Pepi, Vail, Sheika, and Forever.

In 1962, the world renowned ski racer from Austria, Pepi Gramshammer, astonished the skiing world by winning seven of nine professional races to become the biggest money winner of the year. Pepi, who had been a member of the Austrian National Ski Team from 1955 to 1960, became a racing coach and instructor in Sun Valley, Idaho, in 1960. Dick Hauserman, one of the important cogs in the wheel of development of the newly established ski resort of Vail, invited Pepi to experience the Vail terrain. Pepi took a quick tour of the Frontside, and it was love at first sight.

He then decided to ski down the Back Bowls, but there were not yet any lifts to take him back up. He had to climb . . . and climb . . . and climb. The route he took to climb back, and the time he spent in doing so, is commemorated today with the ski run's appropriate name, Forever.

For Pepi, joining the Vail Team was almost like a marriage made in Heaven. But that actual happy event was still to come. In 1963, during racing in Aspen, Pepi met Sheika Moser, also from Austria. They fell for each other almost instantly and married within a year. Together they built the Gasthof Gramshammer, one of the first hotels in the town of Vail. It is patterned after a comfortable old Tyrolean ski lodge and has become a landmark on Bridge Street in the center of the village.

Sheika says, "We're not a five-star hotel. We're a Gasthof." (This statement is perhaps inspired by one of their frequent guests, President Gerald Ford, who often said, "I'm not a Lincoln, I'm a Ford.") However, this Gasthof is certainly in the five-star category. The Gasthof Gramshammer, commonly known as Pepi's, has hosted many celebrities. In addition to President Ford, the names of Leonard Bernstein, John Denver, Jean-Claude Killy, Arthur Ashe, Robert Redford and Barbra Streisand come to mind, along with many others.

Pepi played a prominent role in bringing the World Alpine Ski Championships to Vail and establishing the ski resort as one of the best in North America. As a public relations ambassador for both Vail and Beaver Creek, he was honored by Vail in 1988 when the lower face of International Run was named "Pepi's Face." So there are now two runs that pay homage to his role in Vail's development.

He and Sheika are responsible for bringing a European flavor, particularly Austrian, to Vail Village. Their daughters, Kira and Sheika, are continuing their parents' tradition in the management of Pepi's.

Pepi runs an annual program called Wedel Weeks, which includes instruction in the old Austrian style. A few years ago he and I skied together, and other than commenting favorably on my technique, he didn't try to instruct me. However, he did give me some breathing tips, which have helped my stamina immensely.

Yes, when Pepi joined the Vail Ski Resorts Team, it was very close to a marriage made in heaven. Close, but not close enough. His marriage to Sheika answers that description. It has given still another meaning to "Forever!"

Sheika and Pepi Gramshammer

SUN VALLEY: MAGICAL, MYSTICAL, AND MUSICAL

It has been called an American "Shangri-La." Its claim as a skiing paradise rivals even that of Zermatt. It is heavenly for sure, but its major significance is historical.

In 1935, Averell Harriman, then chairman of the Union Pacific Railroad, enlisted the aid of Count Felix Schaffgotsch of Austria to scour the western United States to locate a spot for a perfect winter resort. After months of searching, Schaffgotsch found an area near Ketchum, an old mining town in central Idaho. He reported back to Harriman that the location had more delightful features for a winter resort than anything he had seen in Switzerland, Austria, or elsewhere in the U.S.

Within seven months, Harriman built the resort of Sun Valley in this majestic setting. His motivation to promote his railroad resulted in Sun Valley becoming the very first destination ski resort in the U.S.

It was an instant success. The glorious mountain terrain and the magnificent Sun Valley Lodge attracted both European nobility and Hollywood royalty. It became a winter playground for much of the film industry. Regulars included Errol Flynn, Clark Gable, Claudette Colbert and Lucille Ball, as well as Ingrid Bergman and Marilyn Monroe. Members of the Kennedy family were frequent visitors.

Its foremost resident was Ernest Hemingway, who called Sun Valley his refuge. He would write all morning and spend the rest of the day hunting and fishing. Gary Cooper, who also skied, was his hunting companion. "Papa" occupied Suite 206 in the Sun Valley Lodge, and it was there that he finished what I've always considered his greatest work, *For Whom the Bell Tolls*. A bronze bust of Hemingway overlooks Trail Creek; one of the most popular ski runs on Baldy, above Warm Springs, bears his name.

The 1941 film *Sun Valley Serenade* was a romantic comedy starring John Payne and Sonja Henie, featuring the Glenn Miller Orchestra, a top favorite in the Big Band days. Nominated for three Academy Awards, it won the Oscar for best original song, *Chattanooga Choo Choo.* And the feature sleigh-ride song, *It Happened in Sun Valley,* rings in my ears whenever I ski there.

Practically the only place you can now see the film is in Sun Valley itself, where it is played on a continuous loop twenty-four hours a day on closed-circuit TV in the Sun Valley Lodge. I saw it first at the age of fourteen during its movie-theatre run, and I promised myself that I would get to Sun Valley. Now whenever I'm there, I watch the film at least once.

There are two mountains for skiing in Sun Valley, set far apart from each other: Dollar Mountain and Bald Mountain (Baldy). Dollar holds the headquarters of the ski school and is a great area for beginners and low intermediates. Baldy is where most of the action is, with great cruising runs for intermediates and some of the most challenging bowls with unending bumps. Once you enter this terrain, there is no escape, with bumps from top to bottom and no outlet to a groomed slope.

Bald Mountain is for good skiers. The ratings of its slopes are severe: green (easy) runs would be blue (intermediate) in any other resort, and some of the blue runs would be black (difficult) elsewhere.

In 1939, the historic restaurant Roundhouse, with spectacular views, was built on Bald Mountain. It was the first of its kind and is still a rarity in the U.S.—a sit-down indoor restaurant as well as an outdoor deck for dining in sunny weather—with table service. You might think you're in the Alps.

In the past, it was very difficult for nonskiers to get to the Roundhouse, since it is midmountain. But under the aegis of Earl Holding, who acquired Sun Valley in 1977, a gondola was inaugurated during the 2009-2010 ski season to bring skiers and nonskiers for midmountain dining, no longer available only to the skiing elite.

Sun Valley can claim several other firsts. Because Averell Harriman couldn't abide his skiing guests taking uncomfortable rope tows to get up the mountain, he instructed the Union Pacific engineers to devise a more comfortable ascent. They applied the same technology used to haul bananas topside, and the result was the first chairlift in the world. Two more firsts for Sun Valley: the world's first ski school, and the world's first child-sized cross-country tracks.

Earl Holding considers Baldy a royal mountain and has built three grand lodges: two at the base (River Run and Warm Springs) and one at the top (Seattle Ridge). He considers them Baldy's crown jewels.

But the undisputed gem of them all remains the Sun Valley Lodge, as it has been since 1936. Its walls are adorned with the photos of celebrity guests, affording delightful time spent identifying the myriad of film stars, politicians, and nobility as you walk through the same halls these legends walked.

There is a formal dining room on the second floor with live music for dancing, unique in ski resorts. For less formal dining there is Gretchen's on the first floor, named for Gretchen Fraser, Sun Valley's Olympic gold medalist. (She did the skiing scenes for Sonja Henie in *Sun Valley Serenade*.)

Across the lobby is the Duchin Lounge, named after the renowned jazz pianist, Eddie Duchin. Duchin's music is a dancer's delight; five nights a week, Joe Fos and his trio carry on this tradition. During our visit last year, Joan and I danced almost every night, often having the dance floor to ourselves.

On the last night of our trip, a young man sitting with a small group at the table behind us leaned over and commented on how well we danced, and asked how long we had been dancing together. I replied, "Forever!" Later, as we were sitting with Joe Fos during the trio's break, the same young man came over and, apologizing for the intrusion, engaged Joe in conversation regarding some technique the pianist had displayed. He told us he came from a musical family, with the piano his instrument of choice, although he wasn't professional. I asked his name, and when he said, "Nicholas Ma," Joe asked if he was related to the world famous cellist, Yo Yo Ma. Nicholas replied, "He's my dad."

Later, when the music resumed, he returned to our table and asked Joan to dance! She was pleasantly surprised, and agreed.

It seemed miraculous and also mystical how this young man, clearly still in his twenties, was able to dance in the style of the 1940s and 1950s with someone nearly three times his age. He displayed an expertise on the dance floor comparable to that of his father with the cello.

I've always known that Joan is an excellent dancer, but I didn't know just how good until I watched her dancing with Nicholas. It seemed as if it was *they* who had danced with each other *forever*.

In Sun Valley, brushing elbows with celebrities and their families is commonplace. It is just a part of the magic and mystique that has made Sun Valley the American Shangri-La.

THE RIGHT TIME AND
THE RIGHT PLACE

How could I have asked for anything more? My introduction to skiing at the age of forty-five was at the right time, and in the Swiss Alps, the right place.

Why was this the right time? Had I been introduced to skiing earlier in life, it probably would have been unaffordable the way I had taken to it. I spared no expense and included the entire family in most activities, from day trips to upstate New York and New Jersey, to weekends in Vermont and two-week trips to the Alps.

Starting in the Alps was all important, but the local day and weekend trips here in the East played a vital role in developing our skills on hard-pack, ice, and yes, even snow.

Comparing skiing in the East of North America to the West has, at times, conjured up thoughts of the various venues in which we went fishing, another favorite family pastime. Skiing in the East was mindful of fishing in a brook, while skiing in the West was more like angling in a large lake. The Alps? Have you ever gone deep-sea fishing in the Atlantic or the Pacific? Well, the Alps, with vast interconnected areas and hundreds of lifts are, literally, oceans and oceans of snowy skiing terrain.

However, it is often said that if you can ski competently in the East, you can ski any place in the world. The East offers every possible challenging condition you will find anywhere: steeps, bumps, chutes, cliffs, hard-pack, ice, narrow trails, crowded slopes, rocks, and grass. Of course, sometimes, there is fresh powder snow but in most areas of the East, it will be skied off in just a few hours after it falls.

So what is it about the East that draws thousands time and again? For one thing, of all the fifty states in the Union, it includes the one which has the most ski areas. No, it's not Vermont, New Hampshire, or Maine; it's not in New England at all. It's New York!

Probably the most prominent ski area in New York State is Hunter Mountain, part of the Catskill range. Known as the Snowmaking Capital of the World, its major appeal is its proximity to the city, leading to its ability to attract large numbers of singles from the New York metro area.

Areas I've skied in the Catskills in the vicinity of Hunter are Belleayre, Windham, and a little known "sleeper," Plattekill, which has only three lifts, but where I never spent as much as three minutes on a lift line. It was very tiring as we were able to make run after run with hardly a stop.

Bridging two states, New York and Massachusetts, is Catamount, partially owned by a member of my tennis club. Michael and I raced there as a father-and-son team and came in second because Michael's father was too slow.

In the East, the best areas I have skied are in Vermont, each area with its own special characteristics:

Bromley Mountain in southern Vermont, called the Friend of the Family, is relaxed and welcoming even on the busiest days of the season.

Mount Snow boasts about its great array of snow guns and its Terrain Parks. Some say its upscale reputation brings crowds of "snooty" New Yorkers!

Stratton Mountain is an elite area with an excellent lift system (state of the art), high-speed quads and six-packs. Known for its exquisitely groomed slopes, it has surprisingly good tree skiing, adding soul to its great heart!

Okemo is also very family friendly. Its rapid rise in ranking has been remarkable. It is now known for its obsessive grooming and excellent snowmaking. A typical comment: "The Mountain is an intermediate's dream, and my family's favorite place."

Stowe, part of seven decades of skiing heritage, is one of the principals in the history of skiing and is known as the Ski Capital of the East. Its great terrain is not only the most challenging in the region, but it has been said that it would match any challenging terrain on the entire continent.

Killington, the "Beast of the East," is located in the heart of Vermont. Some say it's "the big dog among New England's skiing puppies." The largest ski area in the Northeast, it has two hundred trails and thirty-one lifts. Seven separate mountains comprise an immense trail network that, even with a map in hand, forms a puzzling maze to negotiate.

It is the home of the notorious bump run, Outer Limits, on Bear Mountain. Bear Mountain is where both the U.S. and Swedish Ski Teams trained for the Olympics at Lake Placid in 1980.

There was an amusing incident the first time I skied Wildfire at Bear Mountain with my friend Abe, who delighted in his ski partner going first and then, in true *macho* style, overtaking him. About halfway down on Wildfire there is a forty-five-degree bend, a right angle change of direction. Skiing down first, I stopped just after the bend. Abe came hurtling down but the trees blocked his view of me. He made the turn. I defended myself by raising my left arm, and Abe crashed right into my ski pole, nose first. In no time he had two black eyes, giving him the appearance of a raccoon.

Driving home that night, he was pulled over for speeding. The patrolman shone his flashlight on Abe's face and asked, "What happened to you?" Abe quickly responded, "I had an accident. I'm on my way to a hospital." The officer let him go.

If you start skiing as a youngster, Killington's beginner's slope, Snowshed, would be an ideal place to start. If your first skiing is at Catamount you can brag about skiing in two states in one day. If you live in New York City and are in your twenties, Hunter Mountain, so close to the city, might be the area where you don skis for the first time.

Living in Northern California, and in your thirties or forties, you might start at Lake Tahoe in either Alpine Meadows or Squaw Valley. If you're in your fifties or sixties, it might be Heavenly Valley. And if you are seventy, living in Miami Beach and skiing for the first time, you might possibly ski in Vail, Colorado.

Whether you were first enchanted with skiing on a bunny slope in Upstate New York, or became ecstatic in the lee of the Matterhorn in Zermatt, or enraptured riding down Little Cottonwood Canyon after skiing Big Emma in Snowbird, Utah, you will always remember that first time, leading to the fascination that might have become an obsessive passion. No matter when or where that happened, for you, it will always be the right time and the right place.

**The author and his wife, Joan,
in Killington in the early years**

FAMILY TIES AND TRIBUTES

It seems only fitting to end these memoirs with a few words about family and the person through whom my life of skiing began, my Uncle Jack (known in his professional life as Burnet Hershey).

In his early adulthood, Jack Hirsch was a promising young violinist. He looked forward to continuing in the musical tradition of my grandmother's family. Her father and brothers formed the personal string ensemble of King Carol of Romania, the Orchestra Bughici.[1] (Bughici was my grandmother's maiden name.)

(Of course, there is always one in the family who doesn't follow tradition; in this case, it was Simion Bughici. Although a musician like many in the family, he served as foreign minister of Romania from 1952 to 1955, succeeding the notorious "Hatchet Woman," Ana Pauker.)

Unfortunately, a finger on Jack Hirsch's left hand, the fingering hand, became paralyzed, thereby ending his promising concert career. He moved on to another great interest, journalism, and through the years, he worked for such newspapers as *The Brooklyn Eagle*, *The New York Herald Tribune*, and *The New York Times*. He authored a number of books, including *The Odyssey of Henry Ford and the Great Peace Ship*; *The Air Future*; *Soldier of Peace: Dag Hammarskjold*, and a delightful novel, *You Can't Go to Heaven on a Roller Skate*.

Jack was the youngest journalist to attend the Versailles Peace Conference following the First World War. After each session, he gathered all the papers left on the conference table and compiled a twenty-volume

---

[1] Currently, the family musical tradition is carried on by my nephew, Dennis Koster, one of the few concert guitarists in the world known for both Flamenco and classical, both of which he plays at all his concerts. SH

history of the historic event. He donated the only copy that existed to Princeton University, in honor of his good friend, Albert Einstein.

As president of the Overseas Press Club, he was called upon many times to deliver a eulogy for a departed member. He often started with these words: "Death is more universal than life. Everyone dies, but not everyone lives. Not everyone experiences and writes about the world as has this prominent member of our press corps."

If Burnet Hershey had been a skier eulogizing a fellow skier, he might have said, "Death is more universal than life. Everyone dies, but not everyone lives the life of a skier. It is a life of unending delights and challenges, exquisite remembrances, and the sharing of these wonders with so many. Skiing is a step that tests one's strength, ability to endure and to cope with the uncertainties of changing terrain and capricious elements. It is a sensual, exhilarating step that is balletic and artful. It is truly a *giant step* into an everlasting love affair . . . with the world of skiing."

Thanks again, Uncle Jack!

EPILOGUE

Since the beginning of my skiing days some thirty-nine years ago, I have sensed the magic in the air. The stunning snowscapes and awesome mountains, such as the Matterhorn and the Jungfrau, have formed a cascade of visual delights that continue to tweak my memory.

However, for me, the real magic has been more for the ears and the rhythm of the body than for the eyes. When I ski, I hear—and feel—the music!

No, it's not that I am listening to some recording with an iPod or some such device. The music is in my very being.

Perhaps my family's musical heritage has infused me. Though only on a purely amateur level, writing music and lyrics over the years has been a source of recreation for me. However, I can only describe the music I hear and feel when skiing as being on a much higher plane.

Only twelve musical notes comprise all of music. Whether classical, jazz, or rock and roll, it is only these twelve notes that form the basis of all music of the Western world. Those twelve notes, together with the vast array of rhythms and harmony, form what is for me the infinite universe of music.

Throughout this book, I have used the phrase *world of skiing*, but to me, *universe* would be more apt. This universe has its own planets: the never-ending regions of the Alps in Europe, the Andes of South America, the Rockies of the United States and Canada, the Southern Alps of New Zealand, and many, many more. The all-encompassing variety of terrain, weather, snow conditions, and amazing views present skiers with endless amounts of adventure, challenges, and the pure delights of sliding, skidding, floating, and everything in between. The harmony of these elements is incomparable.

Just listen to the sounds of the mountains, the whistling of the wind in the trees, and the whisper of skis in fresh powder. The click-clack of some chairlifts supplies the rhythm for this musical background. In the early days of my skiing in France, Poma lifts were prevalent. I would ride up this drag lift, sitting on a disc with my skis on the snow. I would hear a melody and join in by humming the tune of my favorite aria from Puccini's *La Bohème.*

Of course, rhythm is the linchpin between music and skiing. How can you make a run of short turns through five or six inches of newly fallen snow and not have the melody of Gershwin's *I've Got Rhythm* run through your mind . . . or *Over the Rainbow* when cruising on a blue run after it stops snowing, the sun emerges, and, yes, there is a rainbow?

Some runs are symphonic in scope. When the terrain changes from cruisers to the steeps, to the bumps, and back and forth, the shape and rhythms of your turns will change accordingly, as will the melodies in your head. Off-piste runs such as the Tour de Charvet down to the Cugnai Valley in Val d'Isère, and the Morteratsch Glacier accessed from St. Moritz, are prime illustrations. Groomed runs such as Northwoods in Vail and Regulator Johnson in Snowbird can be considered sonatas if you are alone, or concertos when skiing with a group.

The symbiotic relationship of skiing to music is enhanced by the sensation of dancing. Certainly the acrobatic flips, rolls, jumps, and spins performed in freestyle skiing and in choreographed ski ballet fantasies (think Suzy Chaffee) are great examples. But this is not how recreational skiers use dancing rhythms. It's doing short, quick, parallel turns down the fall line to the rhythms in your head: a Scott Joplin ragtime, or Debussy's *Golliwog's Cakewalk.* You might even see yourself emulating Gene Kelly in any one of his fabulous numbers in *Singin' in the Rain.* Skiin' on the Snow? It all works. You don't have to be a good dancer to be a good skier, but if you feel it, it will add to your pleasure.

As I have passed through my seventies into my eighties, the years have begun to take their toll. They have reduced the number of days and hours I am able to ski and have limited the terrain I can negotiate. Today, black diamond runs are only a sometime thing. Forget the double blacks. I enjoy the cruisers, the blues. Even when I am not on the snow, I think about skiing, remembering the views, the terrains, the adventures, and the challenges. I am blessed. The magic is ageless. I am still skiing. I still hear the music!

WHERE I HAVE SKIED

The following are the areas where I have skied, but not necessarily where I've stayed. For example, although I have skied many times in Cervinia, I've always stayed in Zermatt; I've skied often in Meribel, but stayed in Courchevel. The many times I skied in Corvatsch, Sils, Diavolezza, and Celerina, I stayed in St. Moritz.

NORTH AMERICA

Canada
> Lake Louise
> The Purcells (via helicopter)
> Sunshine Village
> Whistler-Blackcomb

United States
California
> Alpine Meadows
> Boreal Ridge
> Heavenly Valley
> Kirkwood
> Northstar-at-Tahoe
> Squaw Valley
> Sugar Bowl

Colorado
> Aspen Highlands
> Aspen Mountain
> Beaver Creek
> Buttermilk/Tiehack

Copper Mountain
Loveland Basin
Purgatory
Snowmass
Steamboat Springs
Telluride
Vail

Idaho
Sun Valley

Massachusetts
Brody Mountain
Butternut
Catamount
Jiminy Peak

Nevada
Mt. Rose

New Jersey
Great Gorge
Vernon Valley

New Mexico
Santa Fe
Taos

New York
Belleayre
Highmount
Hunter
Plattekill
Windham

Utah
Alta
Brighton
The Canyons
Deer Valley
Park City
Powder Mountain
Snow Basin
Snowbird
Solitude
Sundance

Vermont

Bromley
Killington
Magic Mountain
Mount Snow
Okemo
Pico Peak
Stowe
Stratton
Sugarbush
Wyoming
Jackson Hole

EUROPE

Austria
Alpbach
Bad Gastein
Bad Hofgastein
Dorfgastein
Ellmau
Finkenberg
Fűgen
Gerlos
Hintertux
Hochfűgen
Ischgl
Kaprun
Kitzbűhel
Lech
St. Christoph am Arlberg
St. Jakob am Arlberg
St. Anton am Arlberg
Zell am See
Zell am Ziller
Zug am Arlberg
Zűrs
France
Argentière
Avoriaz
Chamonix

Courchevel (3 levels)
La Clusaz
La Tania
Le Tour
Les Arcs
Les Gets
Les Menuires
Megève
Morzine
Meribel
Saint Martin de Belleville
St,. Gervais (Mont Blanc)
Tignes
Val Thorens
Val d'Isère

Germany

Garmisch-Partenkirchen

Italy

Cervinia
Cortina
Courmayeur
Livigno
Madonna di Campiglio

Switzerland

Adelboden
Arosa
Celerina
Champery
Corvatsch
Crans-Montana
Davos
Diavolezza
Eggli
Engleberg
Grindelwald
Klosters
La Galb
Lenk
Lenzerheide

Les Diablerets
Leysin
Morgins
Mürren
Nendaz
Rougemont
Saanenmöser
Saas-Fee
Samnaun
Schonried
Sils
Siviez
St. Moritz
Verbier
Veysonnaz
Villars
Wengen
Zermatt
Zweisimmen

SOUTH AMERICA

Argentina
Bariloche
Las Leñas
Chile
El Colorado
La Parva
Portillo
Termas de Chilian
Valle Nevado

ZEALANDIA

New Zealand
Coronet Peak
Mount Hutt
The Remarkables

AFTERWORD

Some joyful experiences in life do not fully penetrate one's consciousness. *Love* has aspects of which we are aware, but also has deeper facets that are its essence, often not always fully perceived.

On Father's Day, my son Jamie, mindful of our family's heritage and my love for skiing, presented me with *The Accident,* a book by a renowned Romanian novelist, Mihail Sebastian. It was recently translated by Stephen Henighan, and reviewed as "a *captivating novel* about a love affair."

In the novel, Paul rescues Nora who has been in an accident. As their relationship develops, Nora feels compelled to rescue Paul from a deep depression. She decides to introduce Paul to skiing, and takes him for a holiday to the Transylvanian mountains. His exhilarating skiing experiences help him escape from his depression. The last chapter has this exchange:

> *"Nora, do you think that skiing can save a person? Can it change his life?"*
> *"Dear Paul, I think that our lives are full of bad habits, compulsions, and obsessions. Skiing cleanses us of them."**

These words, reinforced for me as I wrote this book, brought my love for skiing to another level – a reality that has been experienced but had not fully permeated my awareness.

*Reprinted with the permission of Stephen Henighan